ROB BLAKE

PIT BOSS

WOOD PELLET GRILL AND SMOKER BIBLE 2023

2000 Days of Fail-safe Recipes to Get the Right Firing
Point. Become the Unquestioned #1 Pit Master and
Leave Everyone Speechless

TABLE OF CONTENTS

INTRODUCTION

What is a Wood Pellet Smoker-Grill?

The wood pellet smoker grill is the best appliance for backyard cooking. The wood pellet smoker grill consists of a gas grill, a kitchen oven, and a charcoal smoker. As by its name the wood pellets fuel the grill. The food cook on the grill gets infused with the smoke of burned pellets. For the indoor cooking, it also offers a gas grill that has built-in temperature control. To control the cooking temperature, airflow, and fire; the wood pellet smoker grill has an electronic control panel, thus ensuring the food doesn't burn. New and latest models of wood pellet smoker grill also come with heat sensors for a perfect cooking experience.

The basic popularity of wood pellet smoker grill is its ease of use. The wood pellets used in this smoker grill are about a ¼ inch thick and look like pills. These wood pellets are used in a very controlled way to maintain the required cooking temperate. The wood pellets are available in a wide variety such as cherry, apple, hickory, and many more. These different wood flavors provide the vast Variety of smokiness and flavor. The Smokey flavor is absorbed in the food and creates a unique taste and aroma.

The wood pellets are basically added to a special place known as a storage hopper. This maintains the correct quantity to be added, so the perfect temperature for the type of cooking is achieved. It takes almost 20 minutes to get the wood pellet smoker grill ready.

Sometimes seeing so many recipes at a glance can be very overwhelming. This is why we had segmented this cookbook into different segments each spanning recipes of a similar kind. So, go through the book as and when needed and make sure to follow the instructions in the recipe thoroughly.

When you put a smoker to right use and use the best kind of pellets, the flavor induced is so amazing that not only you but every guest who ends up eating the food is sure to be amazed at the exceptional culinary skills which you possess. I've put in a lot of love, effort, and time in this cookbook to make sure that every recipe is as good as I wanted it to be. Of course, like always, most recipes allow you to do a little makeshift if suppose you are missing out on some ingredients. However, in order to get the best results, we want you to stick to the details as closely as it is possible for you.

So, make the most of this amazing cookbook and try these recipes so that you could take your food buds for a real ride.

As you can see from these recipes, the world of smoking is only as limited as your imagination! Sweet, savory, vegetable, mineral, meat- you can smoke almost anything. As you get more comfortable with these recipes, feel free to start experimenting on your own. The basic principles hold true, but your own taste buds can drive you. Good luck and happy smoking!

CHAPTER 1

Basics of Smoking

Various Functions of the Wood Pellet Grill

Probably the most notable features of the wood pellet grill are its versatility and functionality. It takes advantage of direct and indirect heat to cook food in a variety of ways from barbecue, grilling, smoking, baking, roasting, braising, searing to charring.

Although often used interchangeably, barbecuing and grilling are two different techniques. Barbecuing is cooking meat slowly with the hot air within an enclosed surface.

Grilling is the opposite and is done with the lid open and requires a direct heat source underneath the meat. Regardless of what your preference would be, you can easily accomplish both by using a wood pellet grill.

Exposing meat to wood-fired smoke to infuse it with rich flavor is a cooking method called smoking. Smoking is a superb way to preserve food and is practiced for decades and across many cultures.

Choose from among the different wood pellet flavors to pair up with your choice of meat, poultry, or even vegetables.

Baking is another way of cooking that utilizes dry heat in an enclosed space ideal for making bread, pizza, or pastries.

It would seem out of place to bake in a wood pellet grill, but people can attest to the benefits of that added flavor from using wood pellet blends. Indulge in that added layer of lingering taste and aroma you get from using a wood pellet.

Similar to baking, roasting is another cooking method that utilizes dry heat. It is perfect for evenly cooking large portions of meat or poultry.

The combination of the surrounding heat and the reaction between the amino acids and sugars in the food results in a phenomenon called the Maillard reaction. This gives the food its appetizing brown color and is also responsible for the additional burst of flavors.

Braising uses both wet and dry heat methods. The meat is first sautéed over high temperature then placed in the oven with the remaining liquid. The meat is then cooked by the hot air and the liquid is absorbed to add more flavor.

Some wood pellets allow access to the fire pot, so if your dish requires braising, all you need to do is place it over the fire before using the oven-like function of the same grill.

Searing is a cooking method where the surface of the meat is browned over extremely high heat until crusts form. This is often just an initial step to roasting, braising or grilling and can be done with the use of a regular stainless-steel pan or a cast-iron skillet.

To get the best sear for your steak, make sure that the surface is very dry. It is worth knowing that each type of meat sears differently with varied preparations. It is beneficial to research the best technique according to the meat or manner of cooking required by your dish for you to improve your culinary repertoire.

There is a thin line between scorched and charred food. We all have experienced burning meat at some point in our lives when we forget to take it out on time. But isn't charring also burning by definition?

Charring is the deliberate scorching of the surface of the food in a short amount of time. The difference between burning and charring is the intention.

Burnt food is black and extremely bitter. The entire surface has gone way past the point where it caramelizes and has already become carbonized. Some food tastes better when we allow it to burn in some areas. Vegetables like corn, sweet potatoes, peppers, tomatoes, and onions taste better with a bit of charring.

The chemical reactions that take place cause the vegetables to become sweeter and become permeated with a smoky flavor. The same is true when cooking meat. The charred portion on burgers and steaks not only taste great but surely look appetizing as well.

How to Use It Step-by-Step

Most kitchen appliances are easy to operate and ready to use. If you are planning to purchase a wood pellet grill, make sure to go over the user's manual first before you attempt to fire it up.

If you have recently purchased your unit and are looking for a guide, it is useful to learn about the safety precautions as well. Regardless of the make or brand, most wood pellet grills follow the same procedures to get started.

Step 1: Loading the pellet hopper

After reading and following the user's manual on how to assemble your grill properly, it is now time to get your brand-new pellet smoker ready for the long hours of grilling to come.

It is best practice to inspect the wood pellets before you put these in the hopper. Make sure they are dry and in good condition. The hopper is a container with a lid located on either the left or right side of the grill and holds the wood pellets.

Step 2: Checking for proper feeding

First, plug in your pellet grill into an electrical outlet. Locate the ash container and make sure it is in its proper place. Open the ash damper and set the dial to 'feed' before turning on the grill.

The auger will start revolving at this point and will send pellets into the burner or fire pot. Listen to the sound of pellets hitting the can as this means that the auger is working properly. Close the ash damper.

Step 3: Preparing for the first ignition

This step is essential if you are about to use your grill for the first time. This stage ensures that any packing oils left in the grill will be burned off.

First, make sure that your temperature probe is clean and in good condition as any dirt and grease may cause an inaccurate temperature reading and heat fluctuations. Clean it whenever necessary.

Open the grill lid and turn the power on. Set the temperature to 350 degrees Fahrenheit for about 30 minutes to 1 hour. Some models require the 'smoke' setting for the initial burn and different time duration, so make sure to check your manual.

Step 4: Cooking for the first time

Once the required amount of time has passed for the initial burn, it is now time to finally try out the recipes you have been planning to cook on your new pellet grill.

To start, make sure that the temperature stabilizes inside the cooking chamber. Close the lid and choose the temperature setting required for your recipe. This may take around 10-20 minutes or until the blinking green light remains steady. A steady green light means that the required temperature has been reached and you are now ready to cook.

Step 5: Shutting down

Once you are done with using the wood pellet grill, you must follow the process on how to shut down your grill properly.

It is best to make sure that there is no food left on the grates to avoid build-up and to make clean up easier.

Some models already have the 'shut down' or 'shutdown cycle' option. Avoid unplugging or turning off the pellet grill while undergoing the shutdown process to prevent any damage to your unit. Most units will power off on its own after a few minutes following the shutdown process.

Once the power is out, switch the power to 'off' before unplugging your unit from the outlet.

Pros and Cons of Using It

Pros

- Multi-functional – Wood pellet grills can execute various cooking methods all packed into one apparatus.

- Easy to use – Most units have an array of features meant to make cooking more of an art and less of a chore.

- Short pre-heating times – It only takes about 10-15 minutes depending on the heat requirements.

- Food does not get over smoked – It is easy to over smoke your food when cooking with a charcoal or wood grill, but it is hard to do that when using a pellet grill. The secret lies in how the air flows inside the pellet's cooking chamber. Over smoking happens when smoke stays in the same area for too long and produces a substance called creosote that is not only bitter but also numbs the tongue when consumed.

- No flare-ups – "I miss the putting out the flare every two seconds whenever I'm grilling" said no one ever. If you hate flare-ups, getting a wood pellet grill is the way to go.

- Ample choices for wood pellet flavors – Choose from among the many flavors of hickory, maple, oak, cherry, apple, pecan, alder, bourbon, and mesquite. Take it up a notch by experimenting with different combinations of any of these to bring out the best smoky flavors that will make your meals extraordinary.

- Fuel efficient – On a 'smoke' or low-temperature setting, a wood pellet grill will only use 1/2 pound of pellets for every hour of cooking and only 2-1/2 pounds on a high-temperature setting.

- Remarkable temperature controls – Pellet grills come with thermostats that give precise heat readings to make sure that you're cooking your food adequately.

- Great recipes to try – Modern units come with a mobile application with pre-loaded recipes and detailed guides to try on your pellet grill. It also allows users to adjust the temperatures and set alarms when necessary remotely.

Cons

- Price – Wood pellet grills, especially the newer models come with high tech accessories such as wireless connectivity that allows you to control the grill's setting from anywhere in the world. It is also made of great quality stainless steel and is heavy-duty. Pellet grills retail for about $400 and some up to $4000.

- Electricity – We often associate BBQs with camping so if your grill is 100% dependent on electricity this limits your options. Furthermore, electricity costs may be a concern for some people if they are planning to constantly use these pellet smokers for 12 hours or more for slow cooking or smoking.

- Not ideal for use in wet conditions – Wood pellets need to be completely dry to burn well. Moisture can easily cause deterioration to wood pellets if not stored properly. Wood pellet grills, although meant for outdoor cooking, are not waterproof. It has electrical components that may be damaged and can break down over time, which is another significant point to consider.

- Grill marks – If you are expecting to have appetizing sear marks like the ones you get from charcoal and wood grills, you might get disappointed. Wood pellet grills make the most of indirect heat to cook the food. Searing is still possible by heating the grates for at least 20 minutes before pressing it on the meat which may be a bit of work for some.

- When inspecting components or when cleaning your pellet smokers make sure that the unit is unplugged or not connected to an electrical outlet.

- When you plan on cleaning your grills after use, see to it that it has completely cooled down first before attempting to take it apart.

- Follow the shutdown process indicated in the user's manual.

- Make sure that the cords and electrical parts are not exposed to moisture, water, and other liquids such as marinades or sauces.

- When in use, electrical cords should be connected to a ground fault interrupter to avoid damaging your unit in the event of electrical fluctuations or malfunctions.

- Always keep your wood pellets in a secured lidded container to prevent contamination or moisture from compromising the pellets. The hopper is not an ideal place for storing your unused pellets over long periods.

- Use only natural and food-grade wood pellets. Look for reputable brands that your manufacturer recommends for use with their unit.

- Ensure that the knob or switch is in the 'off' position before plugging in and plugging out of a power outlet.

CHAPTER 2

Smoking Meat Basic Tips

Mastering the art of smoking foods makes the objective of every cook around the world. And in order to be able to perfect the smoking foods; there are some basics and instructions each of us needs to follow in order to achieve it.

So now that you are ready to begin, start by lighting your smoker and get started, here are some tips that can help you enjoy the taste you are seeking:

1. **Smoking food needs a low heat and keep it low for a few hours allowing the smoke to penetrate through the meats.**

Maintaining a consistent heat makes a critical factor that can positively affect your smoking process and this process can be quite straightforward. You can use a chimney starter to get your coals to a temperature of about 250° F. And if you don't have a thermometer, the best way to determine the right temperature is to hold your hand on top of the coals.

It is effortless; all you have to do is to pile the coals over the bottom; then add the smoking wood and put the meat onto the grill right into the opposite side of the coals you use. You can always add coals from time to time to maintain the same temperature.

2. **Smoking meat needs patience**

Smoking meat is a long process that needs a few hours. For instance, slow cooking meat through smoking it breaks down the meat into tender pieces and keeps its flavors and juiciness.

There are different types of meat, each type takes between about 5 to 7 hours to be perfectly smoked. Make sure not to peek at your ingredients while it is smoking, except for adding more coals to maintain a balanced temperature or to refill the water pan.

3. Decide whether you want the smoking process to be dry or wet:

The wet smoking process includes a pan filled with water and coals that can create a smoky atmosphere that will help moisturize the meat. You can also use a fruit juice or any other types of equipment's to add extra favors. Wet smoking results in a flavorful bark that people will love.

4. Make sure to choose the right meat for you

Not all types of meat are suitable for smoking meat; turkey and chicken make an excellent meat choice; but since the smoking process takes a long time, the skin won't stand up. Besides, brining will help you through the process of smoking.

5. Using a rub is substantial in any smoking process

Making the rub is very important before smoking food and for a perfect rub you can combine about ½ cup of kosher salt with 1 tablespoon of lemon pepper, ½ cup of brown sugar, 1 tablespoon of black pepper, and about 2 teaspoons of chili flakes; then Rub this mixture over the meat right before you start smoking.

6. Choose the right wood

In order to smoke meat properly you should carefully choose the wood you are going to use. For instance, apple wood will offer you a sweet and fruity smoke that goes very well with pork while using Hickory wood makes a perfect choice that you can use with red meat like ribs. You can use alder meat with poultry, fish and any type of white meat.

Pecan wood burns in a more relaxed way in comparison to other woods and makes a perfect choice to cook pork and brisket roasts. You can also use oak wood, cherry wood and other types of food according to the type of meat and the type of flavor you want to use.

7. The importance of brining in the process of smoking:

Bringing any type of meat can keep it meat keeps it from drying out during the process of smoking food. The salt within the brine can make the used proteins more water-absorbent. Indeed, when the sodium and the chloride ions get into the protein tissue so that they can hold onto the moisture. It is recommended to soak the meat in the brine for about 10 to 12 hours right before smoking it.

CHAPTER 3
Rub and Sauces Recipes

PREPARATION: 15 MIN

COOKING TIME: 1 H 20'

SERVES: 1

1. Smoked Tomato Cream Sauce

INGREDIENTS

- 1 lb. beefsteak tomatoes, fresh and quartered
- 1-1/2 tablespoon olive oil
- Black pepper, freshly ground
- Salt, kosher
- 1/2 cup yellow onions, chopped
- 1 tablespoon tomato paste
- 2 tablespoon minced garlic
- Pinch cayenne
- 1/2 cup chicken stock
- 1/2 cup heavy cream

DIRECTIONS

1. Prepare your smoker using directions from the manufacturer.
2. Toss tomatoes and 1 tablespoon oil in a bowl, mixing, then season with pepper and salt.
3. Smoke the tomatoes placed on a smoker rack for about 30 minutes. Remove and set aside reserving tomato juices.
4. Heat 1/2 tablespoon oil in a saucepan over high-medium heat.
5. Add onion and cook for about 3-4 minutes. Add tomato paste and garlic then cook for an additional 1 minute.
6. Add smoked tomatoes, cayenne, tomato juices, pepper, and salt then cook for about 3-4 minutes. Stir often.
7. Add chicken stock and boil for about 25-30 minutes under a gentle simmer. Stir often.
8. Place the mixture in a blender and puree until smooth. Now squeeze the mixture through a sieve, fine mesh, to discard solids and release the juices,
9. Transfer the sauce in a saucepan, small, and add the cream.
10. Simmer for close to 6 minutes over low-medium heat until thickened slightly. Season with pepper and salt.
11. Serve warm with risotto cakes.

NUTRITION

- Calories 50 calories
- Fat 5g
- Carbohydrates 2g
- Protein 0g
- Fiber 0g

PREPARATION: 30 MIN

COOKING TIME: 1 H

SERVES: 4

2. Smoked Mushroom Sauce

INGREDIENTS

- 1-quart chef mix mushrooms
- 2 tablespoon canola oil
- 1/4 cup julienned shallots
- 2 tablespoon chopped garlic
- Salt and pepper to taste
- 1/4 cup Alfasi Cabernet Sauvignon
- 1 cup beef stock
- 2 tablespoon margarine

DIRECTIONS

1. Crumple four foil sheets into balls. Puncture multiple places in the foil pan then place mushrooms in the foil pan. Smoke in a pellet grill for about 30 minutes. Remove and cool.
2. Heat canola oil in a pan, sauté, add shallots and sauté until translucent.
3. Add mushrooms and cook until supple and rendered down.
4. Add garlic and season with pepper and salt. Cook until fragrant.
5. Add beef stock and wine then cook for about 6-8 minutes over low heat. Adjust seasoning.
6. Add margarine and stir until sauce is thickened and a nice sheen.
7. Serve and enjoy!

NUTRITION

- Calories 300 calories
- Fat 30g
- Carbohydrates 10g
- Protein 4g
- Fiber 0g

PREPARATION: 10 MIN

COOKING TIME: 1 H

SERVES: 2

3. SMOKED CRANBERRY SAUCE

INGREDIENTS

- 12 oz bag cranberries
- 2 chunks ginger, quartered
- 1 cup apple cider
- 1 tablespoon honey whiskey
- 5.5 oz fruit juice
- 1/8 tablespoon ground cloves

- 1/8 tablespoon cinnamon
- 1/2 orange zest
- 1/2 orange
- 1 tablespoon maple syrup
- 1 apple, diced and peeled
- 1/2 cup sugar
- 1/2 brown sugar

DIRECTIONS

1. Preheat your pellet grill to 375oF.
2. Place cranberries in a pan then add all other ingredients.
3. Place the pan on the grill and cook for about 1 hour until cooked through.
4. Remove ginger pieces and squeeze juices from the orange into the sauce.

NUTRITION

- Calories 48 calories
- Total fat 0.1g
- Carbohydrates 12.3g

- Protein 0.4g
- Fiber 2.3g

PREPARATION: 10 MIN

COOKING TIME: 1 HOUR

SERVES: 2

4. SMOKED SRIRACHA SAUCE

INGREDIENTS

- 1 lb. Fresno chilies, stems pulled off and seeds removed
- 1/2 cup rice vinegar
- 1/2 cup red wine vinegar
- 1 carrot, medium and cut into rounds, 1/4 inch
- 1-1/2 tablespoon sugar, dark brown
- 4 garlic cloves, peeled
- 1 tablespoon olive oil
- 1 tablespoon kosher salt
- 1/2 cup water

DIRECTIONS

1. Smoke chilies in a smoker for about 15 minutes.
2. Bring to boil both vinegars then add carrots, sugar, and garlic. Simmer for about 15 minutes while covered. Cool for 30 minutes.
3. Place the chilies, olive oil, vinegar-vegetable mixture, salt, and ¼ cup water into a blender.
4. Blend for about 1-2 minutes on high. Add remaining water and blend again. You can add another 1/4 cup water if you want your sauce thinner.
5. Pour the sauce into jars and place in a refrigerator.
6. Serve.

NUTRITION

- Calories 147 cal
- Fat 5.23g
- Carbohydrates 21g

- Protein 3g
- Fiber 3g

PREPARATION: 15 MIN

COOKING TIME: 1 H

SERVES: 1

5. Smoked Soy Sauce

INGREDIENTS

DIRECTIONS

- 100ml soy sauce
- Bradley flavor Bisquettes Cherry

1. Put soy sauce in a heat-resistant bowl, large-mouth.
2. Smoke in a smoker at 158-176oF for about 1 hour. Stir a few times.
3. Remove and cool then put in a bottle. Let sit for one day.
4. Serve and enjoy!

NUTRITION

- Calories 110 cal
- Fat 0g
- Carbohydrates 25g

- Protein 2g
- Fiber 0g

PREPARATION: 5 MIN

COOKING TIME:30 MIN

SERVES: 2

6. Smoked Garlic Sauce

INGREDIENTS

DIRECTIONS

- 3 whole garlic heads
- 1/2 cup mayonnaise
- 1/4 cup sour cream
- 2 tablespoon lemon juice
- 2 tablespoon cider vinegar
- Salt to taste

1. Cut the garlic heads off then place in a microwave-safe bowl; add 2 tablespoon water and cover. Microwave for about 5-6 minutes on medium.
2. Heat your grill on medium.
3. Place the garlic heads in a shallow 'boat' foil and smoke for about 20-25 minutes until soft.
4. Transfer the garlic heads into a blender. Process for a few minutes until smooth.
5. Add remaining ingredients and process until everything is combined.

NUTRITION

- Calories 20 cal
- Fat 0g
- Carbohydrates 10g

- Protein 0g
- Fiber 1g

PREPARATION:205 MIN   COOKING TIME: 1 H   SERVES: 2

7. Smoked Cherry BBQ Sauce

INGREDIENTS

- 2 lb. dark sweet cherries, pitted
- 1 large chopped onion
- 1/2 tablespoon red pepper flakes, crushed
- 1 tablespoon kosher salt or to taste
- 1/2 tablespoon ginger, ground
- 1/2 tablespoon black pepper
- 1/2 tablespoon cumin
- 1/2 tablespoon cayenne pepper
- 1 tablespoon onion powder
- 1 tablespoon garlic powder
- 1 tablespoon smoked paprika
- 2 chopped garlic cloves
- 1/2 cup pinot noir
- 2 tablespoon yellow mustard
- 1-1/2 cups ketchup
- 2 tablespoon balsamic vinegar
- 1/3 cup apple cider vinegar
- 2 tablespoon dark soy sauce
- 1 tablespoon liquid smoke
- 1/4 cup Worcestershire sauce
- 1 tablespoon hatch Chile powder
- 3 tablespoon honey
- 1 cup brown sugar
- 3 tablespoon molasses

DIRECTIONS

1. Preheat your smoker to 250oF.
2. Place cherries in a baking dish, medium, and smoke for about 2 hours.
3. Sauté onions and red pepper flakes in a pot, large, with 2 tablespoon oil for about 4 minutes until softened.
4. Add salt and cook for an additional 1 minute.
5. Add ginger, black pepper, cumin, onion powder, garlic powder, and paprika then drizzle with oil and cook for about 1 minute until fragrant and spices bloom.
6. Stir in garlic and cook for about 30 seconds.
7. Pour in pinot noir scraping up for 1 minute for any bits stuck to your pan bottom.
8. Add yellow mustard, ketchup, balsamic vinegar, apple cider vinegar, dark soy sauce, liquid smoke, and Worcestershire sauce. Stir to combine.
9. Add cherries and simmer for about 10 minutes.
10. Add honey, brown sugar, and molasses and stir until combined. Simmer for about 30-45 minutes over low heat until your liking.
11. Place everything into a blender and process until a smooth sauce.
12. Enjoy with favorite veggies or protein. You can refrigerate in jars for up to a month.

NUTRITION

- Calories 35 calories
- Fat 0g
- Carbohydrates 9g
- Protein 0g
- Fiber 0g

PREPARATION: 15 MIN

COOKING TIME: 1 H

SERVES: 8

8. SMOKED GARLIC WHITE SAUCE

INGREDIENTS

- 2 cups hickory wood chips, soaked in water for 30 minutes
- 3 whole garlic heads
- 1/2 cup mayonnaise
- 1/3 cup sour cream
- 1 juiced lemon
- 2 tablespoon apple cider vinegar
- Salt to taste

DIRECTIONS

1. Cut garlic heads to expose the inside and place in a container, microwave-safe, with 2 tablespoon water. Microwave for about 5-6 minutes on medium.
2. Preheat your grill. Place garlic heads on a shallow foil "boat" and place it on the grill.
3. Close the grill and cook for about 20-25 minutes until soft completely. Remove and cool.
4. Transfer into a blender then add the remaining ingredients. Process until smooth.
5. Serve immediately or store in a refrigerator for up to 5 days.

NUTRITION

- Calories 20 cal
- Fat 0g
- Carbohydrates 8g

- Protein 0g
- Fiber 0g

CHAPTER 4

Pork Recipes

PREPARATION: 15 MIN

 COOKING TIME: 1 H

 SERVES: 1

5. Smoked Soy Sauce

INGREDIENTS

- 100ml soy sauce
- Bradley flavor Bisquettes Cherry

DIRECTIONS

1. Put soy sauce in a heat-resistant bowl, large-mouth.
2. Smoke in a smoker at 158-176oF for about 1 hour. Stir a few times.
3. Remove and cool then put in a bottle. Let sit for one day.
4. Serve and enjoy!

NUTRITION

- Calories 110 cal
- Fat 0g
- Carbohydrates 25g
- Protein 2g
- Fiber 0g

 PREPARATION: 5 MIN

 COOKING TIME:30 MIN

 SERVES: 2

6. Smoked Garlic Sauce

INGREDIENTS

- 3 whole garlic heads
- 1/2 cup mayonnaise
- 1/4 cup sour cream
- 2 tablespoon lemon juice
- 2 tablespoon cider vinegar
- Salt to taste

DIRECTIONS

1. Cut the garlic heads off then place in a microwave-safe bowl; add 2 tablespoon water and cover. Microwave for about 5-6 minutes on medium.
2. Heat your grill on medium.
3. Place the garlic heads in a shallow 'boat' foil and smoke for about 20-25 minutes until soft.
4. Transfer the garlic heads into a blender. Process for a few minutes until smooth.
5. Add remaining ingredients and process until everything is combined.

NUTRITION

- Calories 20 cal
- Fat 0g
- Carbohydrates 10g
- Protein 0g
- Fiber 1g

PREPARATION:205 MIN

COOKING TIME: 3 H

SERVES: 5

9. SMOKED AVOCADO PORK RIBS

INGREDIENTS

DIRECTIONS

- 2 lbs of pork spare ribs
- 1 cup of avocado oil
- 1 teaspoon of garlic powder
- 1 teaspoon of onion powder
- 1 teaspoon of sweet pepper flakes
- Salt and pepper, to taste

1. In a bowl, combine the avocado oil, garlic salt, garlic powder, onion powder, sweet pepper flakes, and salt and pepper.
2. Place pork chops in a shallow container and pour evenly avocado mixture.
3. Cover and refrigerate for at least 4 hours, or overnight.
4. Start pellet grill on, lid open, until the fire is established (4-5 minutes). Increase the temperature to 225⊠ and allow to pre-heat, lid closed, for 10 - 15 minutes.
5. Arrange pork chops on the grill rack and smoke for about 3 to 4 hours.
6. Transfer pork chops on serving plate, let them rest for 15 minutes and serve.

NUTRITION

- Calories: 677 cal
- Carbohydrates: 0.9g
- Fat: 64g
- Fiber: 0.14g
- Protein: 28.2g

PREPARATION: 15 MIN

COOKING TIME: 1 HOUR

SERVES: 4

10. SMOKED HONEY - GARLIC PORK CHOPS

INGREDIENTS

DIRECTIONS

- 1/4 cup of lemon juice freshly squeezed
- 1/4 cup honey (preferably a darker honey)
- 3 cloves garlic, minced
- 2 tablespoons of soy sauce (or tamari sauce)
- Salt and pepper to taste
- 24 ounces center-cut pork chops boneless

1. Combine honey, lemon juice, soy sauce, garlic and the salt and pepper in a bowl.
2. Place pork in a container and pour marinade over pork.
3. Cover and marinate in a fridge overnight.
4. Remove pork from marinade and pat dry on kitchen paper towel. (Reserve marinade)
5. Start your pellet on Smoke with the lid open until the fire is established (4 - 5 minutes). Increase temperature to 450⊠ and preheat, lid closed, for 10 - 15 minutes.
6. Arrange the pork chops on the grill racks and smoke for about one hour (depending on the thickness)
7. In a meantime, heat remaining marinade in a small saucepan over medium heat to simmer.
8. Transfer pork chops on a serving plate, pour with the marinade and serve hot.

NUTRITION

- Calories: 301.5 cal
- Carbohydrates: 17g
- Fat: 6.5g
- Fiber: 0.2g
- Protein: 41g

PREPARATION: 15 MIN

COOKING TIME: 1 H 45 MIN

SERVES: 4

11. SMOKED PORK BURGERS

INGREDIENTS

- 2 lb ground pork
- 1/2 of onion fincly chopped
- 2 Tablespoon fresh sage, chopped
- 1 teaspoon garlic powder
- 1 teaspoon cayenne pepper
- Salt and pepper to taste

DIRECTIONS

1. Start the pellet grill (recommended hickory pellet) on SMOKE with the lid open until the fire is established. Set the temperature to 225 ⊠ and preheat, lid closed, for 10 to 15 minutes.
2. In a bowl, combine ground pork with all remaining ingredients.
3. Use your hands to mix thoroughly. Form mixture into 8 evenly burgers.
4. Place the hamburgers on the racks.
5. Smoke the burgers for 60 to 90 minutes until they reach an internal temperature of 150 to 160°F.
6. Serve hot.

NUTRITION

- Calories: 588.7 cal
- Carbohydrates: 1g
- Fat: 48.2g

- Fiber: 0.5g
- Protein: 38.4g

PREPARATION: 20 MIN

COOKING TIME: 3 HOURS

SERVES: 4

12. SMOKED PORK CHOPS MARINATED WITH TARRAGON

INGREDIENTS

- 1/2 cup olive oil
- 4 Tablespoon of fresh tarragon chopped
- 2 teaspoon fresh thyme, chopped
- Salt and grated black pepper
- 2 teaspoon apple-cider vinegar
- 4 pork chops or fillets

DIRECTIONS

1. Whisk the olive oil, tarragon, thyme, salt, pepper, apple cider and stir well.
2. Place the pork chops in a container and pour with tarragon mixture.
3. Refrigerate for 2 hours.
4. Start pellet grill on, lid open, until the fire is established (4-5 minutes). Increase the temperature to 225⊠ and allow to pre-heat, lid closed, for 10 - 15 minutes.
5. Remove chops from marinade and pat dry on kitchen towel.
6. Arrange pork chops on the grill rack and smoke for about 3 to 4 hours.
7. Transfer chops on a serving platter and let it rest 15 minutes before serving.

NUTRITION

- Calories: 528.8 cal
- Carbohydrates: 0.6g
- Fat: 35g

- Fiber: 0.14g
- Protein: 51g

PREPARATION: 4 HOURS

COOKING TIME: 1 H 45 MIN

SERVES: 4

13. SMOKED PORK CUTLETS IN CITRUS-HERBS MARINADE

INGREDIENTS

- 4 pork cutlets
- 1 fresh orange juice
- 2 large lemons freshly squeezed
- 10 twigs of coriander chopped
- 2 Tablespoon of fresh parsley finely chopped
- 3 cloves of garlic minced
- 2 Tablespoon of olive oil
- Salt and ground black pepper

DIRECTIONS

1. Place the pork cutlets in a large container along with all remaining ingredients; toss to cover well.
2. Refrigerate at least 4 hours, or overnight.
3. When ready, remove the pork cutlets from marinade and pat dry on kitchen towel.
4. Start pellet grill on, lid open, until the fire is established (4-5 minutes). Increase the temperature to 250⊠ and allow to pre-heat, lid closed, for 10 - 15 minutes.
5. Place pork cutlets on grill grate and smoke for 1 1/2 hours.
6. Serve hot.

NUTRITION

- Calories: 260 cal
- Carbohydrates: 5g
- Fat: 12g

- Fiber: 0.25g
- Protein: 32.2g

PREPARATION: 4 HOURS

COOKING TIME: 1 H 45 MIN

SERVES: 4

14. SMOKED PORK CUTLETS WITH CARAWAY AND DILL

INGREDIENTS

- 4 pork cutlets
- 2 lemons freshly squeezed
- 2 Tablespoon fresh parsley finely chopped
- 1 Tablespoon of ground caraway
- 3 Tablespoon of fresh dill finely chopped
- 1/4 cup of olive oil
- Salt and ground black pepper

DIRECTIONS

1. Place the pork cutlets in a large resealable bag along with all remaining ingredients; shake to combine well.
2. Refrigerate for at least 4 hours.
3. Remove the pork cutlets from marinade and pat dry on kitchen towel.
4. Start the pellet grill (recommended maple pellet) on SMOKE with the lid open until the fire is established. Set the temperature to 250 ⊠ and preheat, lid closed, for 10 to 15 minutes.
5. Arrange pork cutlets on the grill rack and smoke for about 1 1/2 hours.
6. Allow cooling on room temperature before serving.

NUTRITION

- Calories: 308 cal
- Carbohydrates: 2.4g
- Fat: 18.5g

- Fiber: 0.36g
- Protein: 32g

PREPARATION: 15 MIN	COOKING TIME: 3 HOURS	SERVES: 6

15. Smoked Pork Loin In Sweet-Beer Marinade

INGREDIENTS

Marinade
- 1 onion finely diced
- 1/4 cup honey (preferably a darker honey)
- 1 1/2 cups of dark beer
- 4 Tablespoon of mustard
- 1 Tablespoon fresh thyme finely chopped
- Salt and pepper

Pork
- 3 1/2 lbs of pork loin

DIRECTIONS

1. Combine all ingredients for the marinade in a bowl.
2. Place the pork along with marinade mixture in a container, and refrigerate overnight.
3. Remove the pork from marinade and dry on kitchen towel.
4. Prepare the grill on Smoke with the lid open until the fire is established (4 to 5 minutes). Set the temperature to 250F and preheat, lid closed, for 10 to 15 minutes.
5. Place the pork on the grill rack and smoke until the internal temperature of the pork is at least 145-150 ☒ (medium-rare), 2-1/2 to 3 hours.
6. Remove meat from the smoker and let rest for 15 minutes before slicing.
7. Serve hot or cold.

NUTRITION

- Calories: 444.6 cal
- Carbohydrates: 17g
- Fat: 12.7g

- Fiber: 0.8g
- Protein: 60.5g

PREPARATION:205 MIN	COOKING TIME: 3 HOURS	SERVES: 6

16. Smoked Pork Ribs With Fresh Herbs

INGREDIENTS

- 1/4 cup olive oil
- 1 Tablespoon garlic minced
- 1 Tablespoon crushed fennel seeds
- 1 teaspoon of fresh basil leaves finely chopped
- 1 teaspoon fresh parsley finely chopped
- 1 teaspoon fresh rosemary finely chopped
- 1 teaspoon fresh sage finely chopped
- Salt and ground black pepper to taste
- 3 lbs. pork rib roast bone-in

DIRECTIONS

1. Combine the olive oil, garlic, fennel seeds, parsley, sage, rosemary, salt, and pepper in a bowl; stir well.
2. Coat each chop on both sides with the herb mixture.
3. Start the pellet grill (recommended hickory pellet) on SMOKE with the lid open until the fire is established. Set the temperature to 225 ☒ and preheat, lid closed, for 10 to 15 minutes.
4. Smoke the ribs for 3 hours.
5. Transfer the ribs to a serving platter and serve hot.

NUTRITION

- Calories: 459.2 cal
- Carbohydrates: 0.6g
- Fat: 31.3g

- Fiber: 0.03g
- Protein: 41g

PREPARATION: 15 MIN

COOKING TIME: 3 H 20 MIN

SERVES: 6

17. SMOKED PORK SIDE RIBS WITH CHIVES

INGREDIENTS

- 1/3 cup of olive oil (or garlic-infused olive oil)
- 3 Tablespoon of ketchup
- 3 Tablespoon chives finely chopped
- 3 lbs of pork side ribs
- Salt and black pepper to taste

DIRECTIONS

1. In a bowl, stir together olive oil, finely chopped chives, ketchup, and the salt and pepper.
2. Cut pork into individual ribs and generously coat with chives mixture.
3. Start the pellet grill on SMOKE with the lid open until the fire is established. Set the temperature to 250 ⊠ and preheat, lid closed, for 10 to 15 minutes.
4. Arrange pork chops on the grill rack and smoke for about 3 to 4 hours.
5. Allow resting 15 minutes before serving.

NUTRITION

- Calories: 689.7 cal
- Carbohydrates: 2g
- Fat: 65g

- Fiber: 0.1g
- Protein: 35.2g

PREPARATION: 15 MIN

COOKING TIME: 1 H 45 MIN

SERVES: 6

18. SMOKED SPICY PORK MEDALLIONS

INGREDIENTS

- 2 lb pork medallions
- 3/4 cup chicken stock
- 1/2 cup tomato sauce (organic)
- 2 Tablespoon of smoked hot paprika (or to taste)
- 2 Tablespoon of fresh basil finely chopped
- 1 Tablespoon oregano
- Salt and pepper to taste

DIRECTIONS

1. In a bowl, combine the chicken stock, tomato sauce, paprika, oregano, salt, and pepper.
2. Brush generously over the outside of the tenderloin.
3. Start the pellet grill on Smoke with the lid open until the fire is established (4 to 5 minutes). Set the temperature to 250⊠ and preheat, lid closed, for 10 to 15 minutes.
4. Place the pork on the grill grate and smoke until the internal temperature of the pork is at least medium-rare (about 145⊠), for 1 1/2 hours.
5. Let meat rest for 15 minutes and serve.

NUTRITION

- Calories: 364.2 cal
- Carbohydrates: 4g
- Fat: 14.4g

- Fiber: 2g
- Protein: 52.4g

19. APPLEWOOD SMOKED MANGO PORK QUESADILLAS

INGREDIENTS

- 1 tablespoon olive oil
- 1.7 pounds Smithfield Applewood Smoked Bacon Pork Loin Filet cut into little scaled-down pieces
- 1 teaspoon chipotle stew powder pretty much to your taste
- 1 teaspoon smoked paprika
- 4-inch flour tortillas 6-8
- 1 ready yet firm mango, stripped + diced
- 1 cup cooked rice or quinoa
- 2 cups destroyed sharp cheddar
- Cherry tomato salsa:
- 2 cup cherry tomatoes
- 1 jalapeno seeded + hacked
- 1/4 cup new basil cleaved
- 1/4 cup fresh cilantro cleaved
- Juice from 1/2 a lime
- Salt to taste

DIRECTIONS

1. Warmth a heavy skillet over medium heat and include the olive oil. Include the pork and season with chipotle bean stew pepper and paprika. Cook, regularly mixing until the pork is caramelized all finished, around 8 minutes. Expel from the warmth. Expel the pork to a plate.
2. Utilizing a similar skillet, over medium warmth, include a touch of olive oil. Spot 4 tortillas down on a perfect counter, sprinkle each with destroyed cheddar, at that point equally appropriate the rice, and top with the hacked mango pieces. Presently include the pork, cut into little scaled-down pieces. Sprinkle with somewhat more of the cheddar. Spot the tortilla onto the hot frying pan or skillet and spread with the other tortilla. Cook until the base is firm and brilliant dark-colored, at that point tenderly flip and cook for another 2-3 minutes until fresh and bright.
3. Present with the tomato salsa and cut avocado.

NUTRITION

- Calories: 477 cal
- Carbohydrates: 4.5g
- Fat: 14g
- Fiber: 2.4g
- Protein: 50g

CHAPTER 5

Beef Recipes

PREPARATION: 15 MIN

COOKING TIME: 55 MIN

SERVES: 4

20. GRILLED ALMOND-CRUSTED BEEF FILLET

INGREDIENTS

- 3 lbs. fillet of beef tenderloin
- Salt and pepper to taste
- 1/4 cup olive oil
- 1/3 cup onion, very finely chopped
- 2 tablespoon curry powder
- 1 cup chicken broth
- 1 tablespoon Dijon mustard
- 1/4 cup sliced almonds, coarsely chopped

DIRECTIONS

1. Rub the beef tenderloin with salt and pepper.
2. In a bowl, combine olive oil, onion, curry, chicken broth, mustard, and almonds.
3. Rub your beef meat generously with the curry mixture.
4. Start your pellet grill, set the temperature on High and preheat, lid closed, for 10 to 15 minutes.
5. As a general rule, you should grill steaks on high heat (450-500°F).
6. Grill about 7-10 minutes per side at high temperatures or 15-20 minutes per side at the lower temperatures, or to your preference for doneness.
7. Remove meat from the grill and let cool for 10 minutes.
8. Serve hot.

NUTRITION

- Calories 479.33 cal
- Fat 34.54g
- Carbohydrates 4.05g
- Fiber 1.95g
- Protein 36.82g

PREPARATION: 15 MIN

COOKING TIME: 1 HOUR

SERVES: 6

21. GRILLED BEEF EYE FILLET WITH HERB RUBS

INGREDIENTS

- 2 lbs. beef eye fillet
- Salt and pepper to taste
- 2 tablespoon Olive oil
- 1/4 cup parsley, fresh and chopped
- 1/4 cup oregano leaves, fresh and chopped
- 2 tablespoon basil, fresh and chopped
- 2 tablespoon rosemary leaves, fresh and chopped
- 3 cloves garlic, crushed

DIRECTIONS

1. Season beef roast with salt and pepper and place in a shallow dish.
2. In a medium bowl, combine olive oil, chopped parsley, basil, oregano, rosemary, garlic, and oil. Rub the meat with the herb mixture from both sides
3. Bring the meat to room temperature 30 minutes before you put it on the grill.
4. Start your pellet grill, set the temperature on High and preheat, lid closed, for 10 to 15 minutes.
5. As a general rule, you should grill steaks on high heat (450-500°F).
6. Grill about 7-10 minutes per side at high temperatures or 15-20 minutes per side at the lower temperatures, or to your preference for doneness.
7. When ready, let meat rest for 10 minutes, slice and serve.

NUTRITION

- Calories 427.93 cal
- Fat 31.8g
- Carbohydrates 3.78g
- Fiber 2.17g
- Protein 30.8g

PREPARATION: 8 MIN

COOKING TIME: 50 MIN

SERVES: 5

22. GRILLED BEEF STEAK WITH MOLASSES AND BALSAMIC VINEGAR

INGREDIENTS

- 2 1/2 lbs beefsteak grass fed
- Salt and ground pepper
- 2 tablespoon molasses
- 1 cup beef broth
- 1 tablespoon red wine vinegar
- 1 tablespoon balsamic vinegar

DIRECTIONS

1. Place a beef steak in a large dish.
2. Combine the beef broth, molasses, red wine vinegar and balsamic vinegar in a bowl.
3. Cover, and refrigerate for up to 8 hours.
4. 30 minutes before grilling, remove the steaks from the refrigerator and let sit at room temperature.
5. Start your pellet grill, set the temperature on High and preheat, lid closed, for 10 to 15 minutes.
6. Grill about 7-10 minutes per side at high temperatures or 15-20 minutes per side at the lower temperatures.
7. Transfer meat to a serving dish and let rest about 10 minutes.
8. Serve warm.

NUTRITION

- Calories 295.3 cal
- Fat 6.21g
- Carbohydrates 6.55g

- Fiber 0g
- Protein 52.89g

PREPARATION: 4 HOURS 45 MIN

COOKING TIME: 55 MIN

SERVES: 6

23. GRILLED BEEF STEAK WITH PEANUT OIL AND HERBS

INGREDIENTS

- 3 lbs beef steak, preferably flank
- 1 teaspoon sea salt
- 2 tablespoon peanut oil
- 1/4 olive oil
- 2 tablespoon fresh mint leaves, finely chopped
- 2 teaspoon peppercorn black
- 2 teaspoon peppercorn green
- 1/2 teaspoon cumin seeds
- 1 pinch of chili flakes

DIRECTIONS

1. Rub the beef steaks with coarse salt and place in a large dish.
2. Make a marinade; in a bowl, combine peanut oil, olive oil, fresh mint leave, peppercorn, cumin and chili flakes.
3. Cover and refrigerate for 4 hours.
4. Bring the meat to room temperature 30 minutes before you put it on the grill.
5. Start your pellet grill, set the temperature on High and preheat, lid closed, for 10 to 15 minutes.
6. As a general rule, you should grill steaks on high heat (450-500°F).
7. Grill about 7-10 minutes per side at high temperatures or 15-20 minutes per side at the lower temperatures, or to your preference for doneness.
8. Remove flank steak from the grill and let cool before slicing for 10 -15 minutes.
9. Slice and serve.

NUTRITION

- Calories 346.3 cal
- Fat 15.15g

- Carbohydrates 0.21g
- Fiber 0.07g

- Protein 32.38g

PREPARATION: 15 MIN

COOKING TIME: 55 MIN

SERVES: 4

24. GRILLED BEEF STEAKS WITH BEER-HONEY SAUCE

INGREDIENTS

- 4 beef steaks
- Salt and pepper to taste
- 1 cup of beer
- 1 teaspoon thyme
- 1 tablespoon of honey
- 1 lemon juice
- 2 tablespoon olive oil

DIRECTIONS

1. Season beef steaks with salt and pepper.
2. In a bowl, combine beer, thyme, honey, lemon juice and olive oil.
3. Rub the beef steaks generously with beer mixture.
4. Start your pellet grill, set the temperature on High and preheat, lid closed, for 10 to 15 minutes.
5. As a general rule, you should grill steaks on high heat (450-500°F).
6. Grill about 7-10 minutes per side at high temperatures or 15 minutes per side at the lower temperatures, or to your preference for doneness.
7. Remove meat from the grill and let cool for 10 minutes.
8. Serve.

NUTRITION

- Calories 355.77
- Fat 12.57g
- Carbohydrates 7.68g

- Fiber 0.18g
- Protein 49.74g

PREPARATION: 4 HOURS 30 MIN

COOKING TIME: 55 MIN

SERVES: 4

25. GRILLED LA ROCHELLE BEEF STEAK WITH CURRIED PINEAPPLE

INGREDIENTS

- 1 1/2 lbs flank steak
- 1/4 cup olive oil
- 8 oz pineapple chunks in juice
- 3 teaspoon curry powder
- 1 tablespoon red currant jelly
- 1/2 teaspoon salt, or to taste

DIRECTIONS

1. Place the flank steak in a shallow dish.
2. In a bowl, combine olive oil, pineapple chunks in juice, curry powder, red currant jelly and salt and pepper.
3. Pour the mixture over flank steak.
4. Cover and refrigerate for 4 hours.
5. Bring the meat to room temperature 30 minutes before you put it on the grill.
6. Start your pellet grill, set the temperature on High and preheat, lid closed, for 10 to 15 minutes.
7. As a general rule, you should grill steaks on high heat (450-500°F).
8. Grill about 7-10 minutes per side at high temperatures or 15-20 minutes per side at the lower temperatures, or to your preference for doneness.
9. Remove flank steak from the grill and let cool for 10 minutes.
10. Serve hot.

NUTRITION

- Calories 406.26
- Fat 26.1g
- Carbohydrates 10.41g

- Fiber 1.85g
- Protein 32.01g

PREPARATION: 15 MIN

COOKING TIME: 55 MIN

SERVES: 8

26. Grilled Veal Shoulder Roast With Fennel And Thyme Rub

INGREDIENTS

DIRECTIONS

- 3 1/2 lb boneless veal shoulder roast
- 2 tablespoon dried thyme leaves
- 1 fresh fennel, thinly sliced
- 2 tablespoon fresh thyme, chopped
- 3/4 teaspoon kosher salt and ground white pepper
- 4 tablespoon olive oil
- 1/2 cup white wine

1. Place a shoulder roast in a large dish and rub with salt and pepper.
2. In a bowl, combine thyme, fennel, salt and pepper, wine and oil.
3. Rub the meat generously.
4. Start your pellet grill, set the temperature on High and preheat, lid closed, for 10 to 15 minutes.
5. Grill about 25 minutes at high temperatures or to your preference for doneness.
6. Remove the veal chops from the grill. Take their temperature with your meat thermometer. The veal chops should have a temperature of 130 degrees Fahrenheit for medium-rare or 140 degrees for medium.
7. Serve hot.

NUTRITION

- Calories 322.71
- Fat 12.14g
- Carbohydrates 4.64g

- Fiber 1.39g
- Protein 36.23g

PREPARATION: 15 MIN

COOKING TIME: 2 H 45 MIN

SERVES: 8

27. Grilled Veal With Mustard Lemony Crust

INGREDIENTS

DIRECTIONS

- 1 lb boneless veal leg round roast
- 1 tablespoon Dijon-style mustard
- 1 tablespoon lemon juice
- 1 teaspoon dried thyme, crushed
- 1 teaspoon dried basil, crushed
- 2 tablespoon water
- 1/2 teaspoon coarsely salt and ground pepper
- 1/4 cup breadcrumbs

1. Place meat on a rack in a shallow roasting pan.
2. In a small mixing bowl stir together bread crumbs, water, mustard, lemon juice, basil, thyme, and pepper. Spread the mixture over surface of the meat.
3. Start your pellet grill, set the temperature on High and preheat, lid closed, for 10 to 15 minutes.
4. As a general rule, you should grill steaks on high heat (450-500°F).
5. Grill about 7-10 minutes per side at high temperatures or 15-20 minutes per side at the lower temperatures, or to your preference for doneness.
6. Remove veal meat from the grill and let cool for 10 minutes.

NUTRITION

- Calories 172 cal
- Fat 3g
- Carbohydrates 4g

- Fiber 0g
- Protein 30g

28. Beef Tenderloin With Balsamic Glaze

INGREDIENTS

- Balsamic Reduction
- 3-4 tablespoons of butter
- 1/3 cups of brown sugar
- 3 tablespoons of fresh rosemary finely chopped
- 3 cups of balsamic vinegar
- 3 garlic cloves of peeled and crushed
- Salt and pepper
- Beef Tenderloin
- Remove silver skin from the trimmed meat

DIRECTIONS

1. Cook the tail (chain portion) by folding it up to ensure an even grilling. Old, the tail together with toothpicks or a butcher's twine, then season with beef rub.
2. Pre-heat wooden pellet smoker grill to about 250 degrees F. At the bottom of the rack, cook the meat for about sixty minutes. Keep an eye on the loins. Let the tender loins reach an average temperature of 115 degrees.
3. Extract the meat from the grill and let cool off. The next thing is to increase the grill heat to about 500 degrees F to sear. Once this is done, place the meat on the searing rack and sear each side for about a minute.
4. The final temperature of the dish should be about 130 degrees. Extract tenderloin from the grill and allow cooling off on a cutting board. With a sharp chef knife, slice the meat into strips. Take the balsamic reduction and drizzle over meat to get the final product.

NUTRITION

- Calories: 40 cal
- Carbohydrates: 0g
- Fat: 3g
- Protein: 8g
- Fiber: 0g

PREPARATION: 30 MIN

COOKING TIME: 30 MIN

SERVES: 4-6

29. CHIPOTLE RUBBED TRI-TIP

INGREDIENTS

- 1 beef tri-tip
- Extra virgin olive oil
- Your favorite salsa, for serving

For the rub:

- 1 tablespoon coarse salt (kosher or sea)
- 1-1/2 teaspoons Chipotle chili powder
- 1-1/2 teaspoons Oregano, preferably Mexican
- 1 teaspoon granulated garlic
- 1/2 teaspoon ground cumin
- 1/2 teaspoon freshly ground black pepper

DIRECTIONS

1. Fire up your pellet grill to medium-high, preferably at about 225 degrees.
2. You could opt for mesquite or your favorite flavor of pellets.
3. Mix ingredients to make the rub in a small clean bowl, stir until it is well combined.
4. Ensure your hands are clean. Next, place the tri-tip in a baking dish and sprinkle rub all over the sides, using your fingers, pat the rub into the meat. Drizzle some amount of virgin olive oil over mixture and rub.
5. Next, transfer the tri-tip to the grill. Reduce the lid and grill the tri-tip until the grill heats up to 100 degrees. Grill for about one hour. Sometimes, it could take lesser time. Remove tri-tip from grill and place in a plate with a foil covering.
6. Heat grill again till about 600 degrees. When at 600 degrees, switch to Open Flame Cooking Mode. Carefully pull out the grill grates and the Hatch and replace with the Direct Flame Insert.
7. Extract the tri-tip from the foil. Place on sear. Sear the tri-tip until it reaches about 120 degrees. It would be crusty and browned on the outside and rare in the center; 130 degrees for medium-rare (or to taste). Cook the two sides for about 4 minutes, turning with thongs. Transfer the tri-tip to a board and cut.
8. Cool meat for about 2 minutes. With a knife make thin cuts across the grain. Top with your favorite salsa and enjoy.

NUTRITION

- Calories: 50 cal
- Carbohydrates: 4g
- Fat: 8g
- Protein: 7.6g
- Fiber: 3.2g

CHAPTER 6
Lamb Recipes

PREPARATION: 30 MIN	COOKING TIME: 2 H	SERVES: 12

30. ROASTED LEG OF LAMB

INGREDIENTS

- 8 pounds leg of lamb, bone-in, and fat trimmed
- 2 lemons, juiced, zested
- 1 tablespoon minced garlic
- 4 sprigs of rosemary, 1-inch diced
- 4 cloves of garlic, peeled, sliced lengthwise
- Salt as needed
- Ground black pepper as needed
- 2 teaspoons olive oil

DIRECTIONS

1. Switch on the Traeger grill, fill the grill hopper with cherry flavored wood pellets, power the grill on by using the control panel, select 'smoke' on the temperature dial, or set the temperature to 450 degrees F and let it preheat for a minimum of 15 minutes.
2. Meanwhile, take a small bowl, place minced garlic in it, stir in oil and then rub this mixture on all sides of the lamb leg.
3. Then make ¾-inch deep cuts into the lamb meat, about two dozen, stuff each cut with garlic slices and rosemary, sprinkle with lemon zest, drizzle with lemon juice, and then season well with salt and black pepper.
4. When the grill has preheated, open the lid, place the leg of lamb on the grill grate, shut the grill, and smoke for 30 minutes.
5. Change the smoking temperature to 350 degrees F and then continue smoking for 1 hour and 30 minutes until the internal temperature reaches 130 degrees F.
6. When done, transfer lamb to a cutting board, let it rest for 15 minutes, then cut it into slices and serve.

NUTRITION

- Calories: 219 Cal
- Fat: 14 g
- Carbohydrates: 1 g

- Protein: 22 g
- Fiber: 0 g

PREPARATION: 25 MIN

COOKING TIME: 1 H 30 MIN

SERVES: 12

31. GREEK-STYLE ROAST LEG OF LAMB

INGREDIENTS

- 7 pounds leg of lamb, bone-in, and fat trimmed
- 2 lemons, juiced
- 8 cloves of garlic, peeled, minced
- Salt as needed
- Ground black pepper as needed
- 1 teaspoon dried oregano
- 1 teaspoon dried rosemary
- 6 tablespoons olive oil

DIRECTIONS

1. Make a small cut into the meat of lamb by using a paring knife, then stir together garlic, oregano, and rosemary and stuff this paste into the slits of the lamb meat.
2. Take a roasting pan, place lamb in it, then rub with lemon juice and olive oil, cover with a plastic wrap and let marinate for a minimum of 8 hours in the refrigerator.
3. When ready to cook, switch on the Traeger grill, fill the grill hopper with oak flavored wood pellets, power the grill on by using the control panel, select 'smoke' on the temperature dial, or set the temperature to 400 degrees F and let it preheat for a minimum of 15 minutes.
4. Meanwhile, remove the lamb from the refrigerator, bring it to room temperature, uncover it and then season well with salt and black pepper.
5. When the grill has preheated, open the lid, place food on the grill grate, shut the grill, and smoke for 30 minutes.
6. Change the smoking temperature to 350 degrees F and then continue smoking for 1 hour until the internal temperature reaches 140 degrees F.
7. When done, transfer lamb to a cutting board, let it rest for 15 minutes, then cut it into slices and serve.

NUTRITION

- Calories: 168 Cal
- Fat: 10 g
- Carbohydrates: 2 g

- Protein: 17 g
- Fiber: 0.7 g

PREPARATION: 10 MIN   COOKING TIME: 10 MIN   SERVES: 8

32. LAMB CHOPS

INGREDIENTS

For the Lamb:
- 16 lamb chops, fat trimmed
- 2 tablespoons Greek Freak seasoning

For the Mint Sauce:
- 1 tablespoon chopped parsley
- 12 cloves of garlic, peeled
- 1 tablespoon chopped mint
- 1/4 teaspoon dried oregano
- 1 teaspoon salt
- 1/4 teaspoon ground black pepper
- 3/4 cup lemon juice
- 1 cup olive oil

DIRECTIONS

1. Prepare the mint sauce and for this, place all of its ingredients in a food processor and then pulse for 1 minute until smooth.
2. Pour 1/3 cup of the mint sauce into a plastic bag, add lamb chops in it, seal the bag, turn it upside to coat lamb chops with the sauce and then let them marinate for a minimum of 30 minutes in the refrigerator.
3. When ready to cook, switch on the Traeger grill, fill the grill hopper with apple-flavored wood pellets, power the grill on by using the control panel, select 'smoke' on the temperature dial, or set the temperature to 450 degrees F and let it preheat for a minimum of 15 minutes.
4. Meanwhile, remove lamb chops from the marinade and then season with Greek seasoning.
5. When the grill has preheated, open the lid, place lamb chops on the grill grate, shut the grill and smoke for 4 to 5 minutes per side until cooked to the desired level.
6. When done, transfer lamb chops to a dish and then serve.

NUTRITION

- Calories: 362 Cal
- Fat: 26 g
- Carbohydrates: 0 g
- Protein: 31 g
- Fiber: 0 g

PREPARATION:105 MIN

COOKING TIME: 1H 15 MIN

SERVES: 4

33. SMOKED RACK OF LAMB

INGREDIENTS

- 1 rack of lamb rib, membrane removed

For the Marinade:
- 1 lemon, juiced
- 2 teaspoons minced garlic
- 1 teaspoon salt
- 1 teaspoon ground black pepper
- 1 teaspoon dried thyme
- ¼ cup balsamic vinegar
- 1 teaspoon dried basil

For the Glaze:
- 2 tablespoons soy sauce
- ¼ cup Dijon mustard
- 2 tablespoons Worcestershire sauce
- ¼ cup red wine

DIRECTIONS

1. Prepare the marinade and for this, take a small bowl, place all the ingredients in it and whisk until combined.
2. Place the rack of lamb into a large plastic bag, pour in marinade, seal the bag, turn it upside down to coat lamb with the marinade and let it marinate for a minimum of 8 hours in the refrigerator.
3. When ready to cook, switch on the Traeger grill, fill the grill hopper with flavored wood pellets, power the grill on by using the control panel, select 'smoke' on the temperature dial, or set the temperature to 300 degrees F and let it preheat for a minimum of 5 minutes.
4. Meanwhile, prepare the glaze and for this, take a small bowl, place all of its ingredients in it and whisk until combined.
5. When the grill has preheated, open the lid, place lamb rack on the grill grate, shut the grill and smoke for 15 minutes.
6. Brush with glaze, flip the lamb and then continue smoking for 1 hour and 15 minutes until the internal temperature reaches 145 degrees F, basting with the glaze every 30 minutes.
7. When done, transfer lamb rack to a cutting board, let it rest for 15 minutes, cut it into slices, and then serve.

NUTRITION

- Calories: 323 Cal
- Fat: 18 g
- Carbohydrates: 13 g
- Protein: 25 g
- Fiber: 1 g

PREPARATION: 10 MIN

COOKING TIME: 3 H

SERVES: 4

34. ROSEMARY LAMB

INGREDIENTS

- 1 rack of lamb rib, membrane removed
- 12 baby potatoes
- 1 bunch of asparagus ends trimmed
- Ground black pepper, as needed
- Salt, as needed
- 1 teaspoon dried rosemary
- 2 tablespoons olive oil
- 1/2 cup butter, unsalted

DIRECTIONS

1. Switch on the Traeger grill, fill the grill hopper with flavored wood pellets, power the grill on by using the control panel, select 'smoke' on the temperature dial, or set the temperature to 225 degrees F and let it preheat for a minimum of 5 minutes.
2. Meanwhile, drizzle oil on both sides of lamb ribs and then sprinkle with rosemary.
3. Take a deep baking dish, place potatoes in it, add butter and mix until coated.
4. When the grill has preheated, open the lid, place lamb ribs on the grill grate along with potatoes in the baking dish, shut the grill and smoke for 3 hours until the internal temperature reaches 145 degrees F.
5. Add asparagus into the baking dish in the last 20 minutes and, when done, remove baking dish from the grill and transfer lamb to a cutting board.
6. Let lamb rest for 15 minutes, cut it into slices, and then serve with potatoes and asparagus.

NUTRITION

- Calories: 355 Cal
- Fat: 12.5 g
- Carbohydrates: 25 g
- Protein: 35 g
- Fiber: 6 g

PREPARATION: 10 MIN

COOKING TIME: 50 MIN

SERVES: 4

35. LAMB CHOPS WITH ROSEMARY AND OLIVE OIL

INGREDIENTS

- 12 Lamb loin chops, fat trimmed
- 1 tablespoon chopped rosemary leaves
- Salt as needed for dry brining
- Jeff's original rub as needed
- ¼ cup olive oil

DIRECTIONS

1. Take a cookie sheet, place lamb chops on it, sprinkle with salt, and then refrigerate for 2 hours.
2. Meanwhile, take a small bowl, place rosemary leaves in it, stir in oil and let the mixture stand for 1 hour.
3. When ready to cook, switch on the Traeger grill, fill the grill hopper with apple-flavored wood pellets, power the grill on by using the control panel, select 'smoke' on the temperature dial, or set the temperature to 225 degrees F and let it preheat for a minimum of 5 minutes.
4. Meanwhile, brush rosemary-oil mixture on all sides of lamb chops and then sprinkle with Jeff's original rub.
5. When the grill has preheated, open the lid, place lamb chops on the grill grate, shut the grill and smoke for 50 minutes until the internal temperature of lamb chops reach to 138 degrees F.
6. When done, wrap lamb chops in foil, let them rest for 7 minutes and then serve.

NUTRITION

- Calories: 171.5 Cal
- Fat: 7.8 g
- Carbohydrates: 0.4 g
- Protein: 23.2 g
- Fiber: 0.1 g

PREPARATION: 10 MIN

COOKING TIME: 4 H

SERVES: 4

36. BONELESS LEG OF LAMB

INGREDIENTS

- 2 1/2 pounds leg of lamb, boneless, fat trimmed

For the Marinade:
- 2 teaspoons minced garlic
- 1 tablespoon ground black pepper
- 2 tablespoons salt
- 1 teaspoon thyme
- 2 tablespoons oregano
- 2 tablespoons olive oil

DIRECTIONS

1. Take a small bowl, place all the ingredients for the marinade in it and then stir until combined.
2. Rub the marinade on all sides of lamb, then place it in a large sheet, cover with a plastic wrap and marinate for a minimum of 1 hour in the refrigerator.
3. When ready to cook, switch on the Traeger grill, fill the grill hopper with apple-flavored wood pellets, power the grill on by using the control panel, select 'smoke' on the temperature dial, or set the temperature to 250 degrees F and let it preheat for a minimum of 5 minutes.
4. Meanwhile,
5. When the grill has preheated, open the lid, place the lamb on the grill grate, shut the grill and smoke for 4 hours until the internal temperature reaches 145 degrees F.
6. When done, transfer lamb to a cutting board, let it stand for 10 minutes, then carve it into slices and serve.

NUTRITION

- Calories: 213 Cal
- Fat: 9 g
- Carbohydrates: 1 g
- Protein: 29 g
- Fiber: 0 g

PREPARATION: 8-10 MIN

COOKING TIME: 1 HOUR

SERVES: 2

37. SUCCULENT LAMB SHANK

INGREDIENTS

- 2 (1¼-pound) lamb shanks
- 1-2 cups water
- ½ cup brown sugar
- ½ cup rice wine
- ½ cup soy sauce
- 3 tablespoons dark sesame oil
- 4 (1½x½-inch) orange zest strips
- 2 (3-inch long) cinnamon sticks
- 1½ teaspoon Chinese five spice powder

DIRECTIONS

1. Preheat the pallet grill to 225-250 degrees F.
2. With a sharp knife, pierce each lamb shank at many places.
3. In a bowl, add remaining all ingredients and mix till sugar is dissolved.
4. In a large roasting pan, place lamb shanks and top with sugar mixture evenly.
5. Place the foil pan in pallet grill and cook for about 8-10 hours, flipping after every 30 minutes. (If required, add enough water to keep the liquid ½-inch over).

NUTRITION

- Calories: 1507 cal
- Fat: 62g
- Carbohydrates: 68.7g
- Fiber: 5g
- Protein: 163.3g

44

CHAPTER 7
Turkey Recipes

PREPARATION: 20 MIN +
MARINATING TIME: OVERNIGHT

COOKING TIME: 3½ TO 4 HOURS

SERVES: 4-5

38. TEMPTING TARRAGON TURKEY BREASTS

INGREDIENTS

For the marinade

- ¾ cup heavy (whipping) cream
- ¼ cup Dijon mustard
- ¼ cup dry white wine
- 2 tablespoons olive oil
- ½ cup chopped scallions, both white and green parts, divided
- 3 tablespoons fresh tarragon, finely chopped
- 6 garlic cloves, coarsely chopped
- 1 teaspoon salt
- 1 teaspoon freshly ground black pepper

For the turkey:

- 1 (6- to 7-pound) bone-in turkey breast
- ¼ cup (½ stick) unsalted butter, melted

DIRECTIONS

To make the marinade

1. In a large bowl, whisk together the cream, mustard, wine, and olive oil until blended.
2. Stir in ¼ cup of scallions and the tarragon, garlic, salt, and pepper.
3. Rub the marinade all over the turkey breast and under the skin. Cover and refrigerate overnight.

To make the turkey

4. Following the manufacturer's specific start-up procedure, preheat the smoker to 250°F, and add apple or mesquite wood.
5. Remove the turkey from the refrigerator and place it directly on the smoker rack. Do not rinse it.
6. Smoke the turkey for 3½ to 4 hours (about 30 minutes per pound), basting it with the butter twice during smoking, until the skin is browned and the internal temperature registers 165°F.
7. Remove the turkey from the heat and let it rest for 10 minutes.
8. Sprinkle with the remaining scallions before serving.

NUTRITION

- Calories: 165 cal
- Fat: 14g
- Carbohydrates: 0.5g
- Fiber: 0 g
- Protein: 15.2g

PREPARATION: 20 MIN

COOKING TIME: 6 HOURS

SERVES: 8

39. Juicy Beer Can Turkey

INGREDIENTS

For the rub

- 4 garlic cloves, minced
- 2 teaspoons dry ground mustard
- 2 teaspoons smoked paprika
- 2 teaspoons salt
- 2 teaspoons freshly ground black pepper
- 1 teaspoon ground cumin
- 1 teaspoon ground turmeric
- 1 teaspoon onion powder
- ½ teaspoon sugar

For the turkey

- 1 (10-pound) fresh whole turkey, neck, giblets, and gizzard removed and discarded
- 3 tablespoons olive oil
- 1 large, wide (24-ounce) can of beer, such as Foster's
- 4 dried bay leaves
- 2 teaspoons ground sage
- 2 teaspoons dried thyme
- ¼ cup (½ stick) unsalted butter, melted

DIRECTIONS

To make the rub

1. Following the manufacturer's specific start-up procedure, preheat the smoker to 250°F, and add cherry, peach, or apricot wood.
2. In a small bowl, stir together the garlic, mustard, paprika, salt, pepper, cumin, turmeric, onion powder, and sugar.

To make the turkey

3. Rub the turkey inside and out with the olive oil.
4. Apply the spice rub all over the turkey.
5. Pour out or drink 12 ounces of the beer.
6. Using a can opener, remove the entire top of the beer can.
7. Add the bay leaves, sage, and thyme to the beer.
8. Place the can of beer upright on the smoker grate. Carefully fit the turkey over it until the entire can is inside the cavity and the bird stands by itself. Prop the legs forward to aid in stability.
9. Smoke the turkey for 6 hours, basting with the butter every other hour.
10. Remove the turkey from the heat when the skin is browned and the internal temperature registers 165°F. Remove the beer can very carefully—it will be slippery, and the liquid inside extremely hot. Discard the liquid, and recycle the can.
11. Let the turkey rest for 20 minutes before carving.

NUTRITION

- Calories: 300 cal
- Fat: 12g
- Carbohydrates: 1g
- Fiber: 0g
- Protein: 42g

**PREPARATION: 20 MIN +
BRINING TIME: OVERNIGHT**

COOKING TIME: 4-5 HOURS

SERVES: 4

40. SMOKED TURKEY LEGS

INGREDIENTS

For the brine
- 1 gallon hot water
- 1 cup curing salt (such as Morton Tender Quick) or kosher salt (see tip)
- ½ cup firmly packed brown sugar
- 2 tablespoons onion powder
- 2 tablespoons garlic powder
- 2 teaspoons freshly ground black pepper, divided
- 2 teaspoons liquid smoke (see tip)

For the turkey legs
- 4 turkey legs
- 1 tablespoon olive oil
- 1 teaspoon salt
- ½ cup Alabama White Sauce, for serving

DIRECTIONS

To make the brine
1. In a large container with a lid, combine the water, salt, brown sugar, onion powder, garlic powder, 1 teaspoon of pepper, and the liquid smoke. Stir until everything is dissolved.
2. Submerge the turkey legs in the seasoned brine, cover, and refrigerate overnight.

To make the turkey legs
3. Following the manufacturer's specific start-up procedure, preheat the smoker to 225°F, and add apple wood.
4. Remove the turkey legs from the brine, and discard the remaining brine.
5. Rinse the turkey legs well and pat dry with a paper towel.
6. Rub the turkey legs with olive oil, and sprinkle with the salt and the remaining 1 teaspoon of pepper.
7. Place the legs directly on the smoker rack and smoke for 4 to 5 hours, until the skin is dark brown and the internal temperature registers 165°F.
8. Remove the turkey legs from the heat and let rest for about 5 minutes.
9. Serve the legs with the Alabama White Sauce on the side.

NUTRITION

- Calories: 120 cal
- Fat: 3g
- Carbohydrates: 0g
- Fiber: 0 g
- Protein: 22g

PREPARATION: 25 MIN

COOKING TIME: 5-6 HOURS

SERVES: 12-14

41. BUTTERED THANKSGIVING TURKEY

INGREDIENTS

- 1 whole turkey (make sure the turkey is not pre-brined)
- 2 batches Garlic Butter Injectable
- 3 tablespoons olive oil
- 1 batch Chicken Rub
- 2 tablespoons butter

DIRECTIONS

1. Supply your smoker with wood pellets and follow the manufacturer's specific start-up procedure. Preheat the grill, with the lid closed, to 180°F.
2. Inject the turkey throughout with the garlic butter injectable. Coat the turkey with olive oil and season it with the rub. Using your hands, work the rub into the meat and skin.
3. Place the turkey directly on the grill grate and smoke for 3 or 4 hours (for an 8- to 12-pound turkey, cook for 3 hours; for a turkey over 12 pounds, cook for 4 hours), basting it with butter every hour.
4. Increase the grill's temperature to 375°F and continue to cook until the turkey's internal temperature reaches 170°F.
5. Remove the turkey from the grill and let it rest for 10 minutes, before carving and serving.

NUTRITION

- Calories: 97cal
- Fat: 4 g
- Protein: 13 g
- Carbohydrates: 1 g
- Fiber: 0 g

PREPARATION: 10 MIN

COOKING TIME: 7 H 30 MIN

SERVES: 10

42. WHOLE TURKEY

INGREDIENTS

- 1 frozen whole turkey, giblets removed, thawed
- 2 tablespoons orange zest
- 2 tablespoons chopped fresh parsley
- 1 teaspoon salt
- 2 tablespoons chopped fresh rosemary
- 1 teaspoon ground black pepper
- 2 tablespoons chopped fresh sage
- 1 cup butter, unsalted, softened, divided
- 2 tablespoons chopped fresh thyme
- ½ cup water
- 14.5-ounce chicken broth

DIRECTIONS

1. Open hopper of the smoker, add dry pallets, make sure ash-can is in place, then open the ash damper, power on the smoker and close the ash damper.
2. Set the temperature of the smoker to 180 degrees F, let preheat for 30 minutes or until the green light on the dial blinks that indicate smoker has reached to set temperature.
3. Meanwhile, prepare the turkey and for this, tuck its wings under it by using kitchen twine.
4. Place ½ cup butter in a bowl, add thyme, parsley, sage, orange zest, and rosemary, stir well until combined and then brush this mixture generously on the inside and outside of the turkey and season the external of turkey with salt and black pepper.
5. Place turkey on a roasting pan, breast side up, pour in broth and water, add the remaining butter in the pan, then place the pan on the smoker grill and shut with lid.
6. Smoke the turkey for 3 hours, then increase the temperature to 350 degrees F and continue smoking the turkey for 4 hours or until thoroughly cooked. The internal temperature of the turkey reaches to 165 degrees F, basting turkey with the dripping every 30 minutes, but not in the last hour.
7. When done, remove the roasting pan from the smoker and let the turkey rest for 20 minutes.
8. Carve turkey into pieces and serve.

NUTRITION

- Calories: 146 cal
- Fat: 8 g
- Protein: 18 g
- Carbohydrates: 1 g
- Fiber: 0 g

PREPARATION: 24 H 10 MIN

COOKING TIME: 5 H 45 MIN

SERVES: 4

43. TURKEY LEGS

INGREDIENTS

- 4 turkey legs
- 1/2 cup curing salt
- 1 tablespoon whole black peppercorns
- 1/2 cup brown sugar
- 1 cup BBQ rub
- 2 bay leaves
- 2 teaspoons liquid smoke
- 4 quarts water, warm
- 2 quarts water, cold
- 4 cups ice

DIRECTIONS

1. Prepare the brine and for this, place a large pot over medium heat, add all the ingredients except for cold water, ice and turkey leg, stir until just mixed, then place the pot over high heat and bring the brine to boil.
2. Then remove the pot from heat, cool the brine at the room temperature, then pour in cold water, add ice and chill the brine in the refrigerator.
3. Add the turkey legs in the brine and let soak in the refrigerator for 24 hours.
4. Then remove turkey legs from brine, rinse well, pat dry and set aside until required.
5. Open hopper of the smoker, add dry pallets, make sure ash-can is in place, then open the ash damper, power on the smoker and close the ash damper.
6. Set the temperature of the smoker to 250 degrees F, let preheat for 30 minutes or until the green light on the dial blinks that indicate smoker has reached to set temperature.
7. Place the turkey legs on the smoker grill, shut with lid and smoke for 5 hours or until nicely deep brown and the internal temperature of turkey reach to 165 degrees F.
8. Serve straight away.

NUTRITION

- Calories: 589 cal
- Fat: 27.7 g
- Protein: 78.7 g
- Carbohydrates: 0 g
- Fiber: 0 g

PREPARATION: 15 MIN

COOKING TIME: 4 H 10 MIN

SERVES: 6

44. JALAPENO INJECTION TURKEY

INGREDIENTS

- 15 pounds whole turkey, giblet removed
- ½ of medium red onion, peeled and minced
- 8 jalapeño peppers
- 2 tablespoons minced garlic
- 4 tablespoons garlic powder
- 6 tablespoons Italian seasoning
- 1 cup butter, softened, unsalted
- ¼ cup olive oil
- 1 cup chicken broth

DIRECTIONS

1. Open hopper of the smoker, add dry pallets, make sure ash-can is in place, then open the ash damper, power on the smoker and close the ash damper.
2. Set the temperature of the smoker to 200 degrees F, let preheat for 30 minutes or until the green light on the dial blinks that indicate smoker has reached to set temperature.
3. Meanwhile, place a large saucepan over medium-high heat, add oil and butter and when the butter melts, add onion, garlic, and peppers and cook for 3 to 5 minutes or until nicely golden brown.
4. Pour in broth, stir well, let the mixture boil for 5 minutes, then remove pan from the heat and strain the mixture to get just liquid.
5. Inject turkey generously with prepared liquid, then spray the outside of turkey with butter spray and season well with garlic and Italian seasoning.
6. Place turkey on the smoker grill, shut with lid, smoke for 30 minutes, then increase the temperature to 325 degrees F and continue smoking the turkey for 3 hours or until the internal temperature of turkey reach to 165 degrees F.
7. When done, transfer turkey to a cutting board, let rest for 5 minutes, then carve into slices and serve.

NUTRITION

- Calories: 131 cal
- Fat: 7 g
- Protein: 13 g
- Carbohydrates: 3 g
- Fiber: 0.7 g

CHAPTER 8
Chicken Recipes

PREPARATION: 10 MIN

COOKING TIME: 2 H 30 MIN

SERVES: 5

45. SMOKED CHICKEN DRUMSTICKS

INGREDIENTS

- 10 chicken drumsticks
- 2 teaspoon garlic powder
- 1 teaspoon salt
- 1 teaspoon onion powder
- 1/2 teaspoon ground black pepper
- ½ teaspoon cayenne pepper
- 1 teaspoon brown sugar
- 1/3 cup hot sauce
- 1 teaspoon paprika
- ½ teaspoon thyme

DIRECTIONS

1. In a mixing large bowl, combine the garlic powder, sugar, hit sauce, paprika, thyme, cayenne, salt, ground pepper. Add the drumsticks, toss to combine.
2. Cover the bowl and refrigerate for 1 hour.
3. Remove the drumsticks from the marinade and let them sit for about 1 hour, until they are at room temperature.
4. Arrange the drumsticks into a rack.
5. Start your pellet grill on smoke, leaving the lid opened for 5 minutes for fire to start.
6. Close the lid and preheat grill to 250°F, using hickory or apple hardwood pellets.
7. Place the rack on the grill and smoke drumsticks for 2 hours 30 minutes, or until the internal temperature of the drumsticks reaches 180°F
8. Remove drumsticks from heat and let them rest for a few minutes.

NUTRITION

- Calories 167 cal
- Fat 5.4g

- Carbohydrates 2.6g
- Fiber 0.5g

- Protein 25.7g

PREPARATION: 15 MIN

COOKING TIME: 2 H

SERVES: 8

46. SMOKED CHICKEN LEG QUARTERS

INGREDIENTS

- 8 chicken leg quarters
- 2 tablespoon olive oil
- 1 teaspoon salt or to taste
- ½ teaspoon chili powder
- ½ teaspoon paprika
- ½ teaspoon ground thyme
- 1 teaspoon dried rosemary
- ½ teaspoon cayenne pepper
- 1 teaspoon garlic powder
- 1 teaspoon onion powder

DIRECTIONS

1. To make rub, combine cayenne, rosemary, garlic, onion powder, chili, paprika, salt, thyme.
2. Drizzle oil over the chicken leg quarters and season the quarters generously with rub mix.
3. Preheat the grill to 180°F with lid closed for 15 minutes, using apple hardwood pellets.
4. Arrange the chicken onto the grill grate. Smoke for 1 hour, flipping halfway through.
5. Increase the grill temperature to 350°F. Cook for an additional 1 hour, or until the temperature of the chicken quarters reaches 165°F.
6. Remove chicken from grill, let it rest for about 15 minutes.

NUTRITION

- Calories 34 cal
- Fat 3.6g

- Carbohydrates 0.9g
- Fiber 0.3g

- Protein 0.2g

PREPARATION: 10 MIN

COOKING TIME: 20 MIN

SERVES: 4

47. Chicken Fajitas

INGREDIENTS

- 2 pounds chicken breast
- 1 large onion (sliced)
- 2 celery stalks (diced)
- 1 large red bell pepper (sliced)
- 1 large orange bell pepper (sliced)
- 1 green bell pepper (sliced)
- 2 tablespoon lime juice
- 2 teaspoon cumin
- 2 teaspoon chili powder
- 1 teaspoon brown sugar
- ½ teaspoon paprika
- 1 tablespoon olive oil
- 1 teaspoon salt
- ½ teaspoon ground black pepper

DIRECTIONS

1. In a large mixing bowl, combine the cumin, lime juice, salt, black pepper, paprika and sugar. Add the chicken breasts and toss to combine. Cover the bowl tightly with aluminum foil, refrigerate for 1 hour.
2. Remove the chicken from the marinade and let it rest for about 1 hour, or until it is at room temperature.
3. Preheat your grill to HIGH with lid closed for 15 minutes.
4. Place a skillet on the grill grate, add the oil.
5. Once the oil is hot, add the onion, celery, red bell pepper, orange pepper, green bell pepper. Sauté until veggies are tender.
6. Remove skillet from heat and cover it to keep the veggies warm.
7. Arrange the chicken breasts onto the grill grate. Cook for about 12 minutes, 6 minutes per side, or until the internal temperature of the chicken breasts reaches 165°F.
8. Remove the chicken from heat and let it rest for a few minutes.
9. Slice chicken breast into thin pieces.
10. Serve with the sautéed vegetables and tortilla.

NUTRITION

- Calories 346 cal
- Fat 9.9g
- Carbohydrates 13.2g
- Fiber 3.1g
- Protein 49.9g

| PREPARATION: 15 MIN | COOKING TIME: 12 MIN | SERVES: 5 |

48. GRILLED CHICKEN KEBABS

INGREDIENTS

- 1 ½ pounds boneless skinless chicken thighs (Cut into 2-inch cubes)
- 1 large bell pepper (sliced)
- 1 large yellow bell pepper (sliced)
- 1 large green bell pepper (sliced)
- 1 onion (sliced)
- 10 medium cremini mushrooms (destemmed and halved)
- Wooden or bamboo skewers (soaked in water for 30 minutes, at least)
- Marinade:
- 2 tablespoon honey
- 1 teaspoon Italian seasoning
- 2 tablespoon finely chopped fresh parsley
- 2 teaspoon finely chopped fresh thyme
- ½ teaspoon ground black pepper
- ½ cup olive oil
- ½ teaspoon salt or to taste
- 1 lemon (juiced)
- ½ teaspoon cayenne pepper

DIRECTIONS

1. In a large mixing bowl, combine all the marinade ingredients. Add the chicken and mushroom. Toss to combine. Cover the bowl tightly with aluminum foil and refrigerate for 45 minutes.
2. Remove the mushroom and chicken from the marinade.
3. Thread the bell peppers, onion, mushroom, chicken unto skewers to make kabobs.
4. Preheat your grill to HIGH with lid closed for 15 minutes, using mesquite hardwood pellets.
5. Arrange the kebobs onto the grill grate and grill for 12 minutes, 6 minutes per side.
6. Remove kebabs from heat.

NUTRITION

- Calories 419 cal
- Fat 25.7g
- Carbohydrates 13.8g
- Fiber 3g
- Protein 34.6g

PREPARATION: 15 MIN

COOKING TIME: 45 MIN

SERVES: 6

49. CHICKEN ENCHILADAS

INGREDIENTS

- 2 pounds shredded chicken
- 1 tablespoon olive oil
- ½ tablespoon taco seasoning
- 1 teaspoon salt
- 1 teaspoon onion powder
- 1 teaspoon ground black pepper
- ½ teaspoon garlic powder
- 1 can (28 ounces) enchilada sauce
- 1 onion (diced)
- 2 cups Mexican blend shredded cheese
- 8 large flour tortilla
- 1 cup sour cream
- 1 (7 ounces) diced green chili
- 2 tablespoon cilantro (chopped)

DIRECTIONS

1. In a large mixing bowl, combine the shredded chicken, sour cream, onion, 1 cup shredded cheese, green chilies, onion powder, taco seasoning, pepper, garlic powder.
2. Spoon equal amount of the chicken mixture into each tortilla and roll.
3. Arrange the stuffed tortilla into a 9-inch by 13-iinch greased baking pan.
4. Pour the enchilada sauce over the tortilla and top with the remaining 1 cup cheese. Cover the pan tightly with aluminum foil.
5. Preheat your grill to 350°F with lid closed for 15 minutes, using mesquite hardwood pellets.
6. Place the pan on the grill and cook for 30 minutes.
7. Uncover the pan and cook for an additional 1 hour.
8. Remove pan from heat, let the enchilada rest for a few minutes.
9. Cut into sizes. Serve and garnish with chopped cilantro.

NUTRITION

- Calories 546 cal
- Fat 25.3g
- Carbohydrates 22.6g
- Fiber 2.6g
- Protein 55.2g

50. Honey Baked Mustard Chicken

INGREDIENTS

- 4 boneless skinless chicken breasts (4 ounces each)
- 1 tablespoon grainy mustard
- 4 tablespoon honey
- ½ teaspoon white vinegar
- ½ teaspoon paprika
- 2 tablespoon Dijon mustard
- 1 tablespoon + 2 teaspoon olive oil
- 1 teaspoon salt
- 1 teaspoon ground black pepper or to taste
- 1 tablespoon freshly chopped parsley
- 1 teaspoon dried basil

DIRECTIONS

1. Preheat the wood pellet grill to 375°F with lid closed for 15 minutes.
2. Grease a baking dish with a non-sticky cooking spray.
3. Season both sides of the chicken breasts with pepper and salt.
4. Place a cast iron skillet on the grill and add 2 teaspoon olive oil.
5. Once the oil is hot, add the seasoned chicken breast, sauté until both sides of the chicken breasts are browned.
6. Use a slotted spoon to transfer the fried chicken breast to a paper towel lined plate.
7. Combine the Dijon mustard, honey, vinegar, basil, grainy mustard, remaining oil, paprika in a mixing bowl. Mix until the ingredients are well combined.
8. Pour half of the honey mixture into the prepared baking dish, spread it to cover the bottom of the dish.
9. Arrange the chicken breast into the dish and pour the remaining honey mixture over the chicken.
10. Cover the baking dish with foil and place it on the grill. Cook on grill for about 20 minutes.
11. Remove the foil cover and cook, uncovered, for 15 minutes.
12. Remove the baking dish from the grill and let the chicken cool for a few minutes.

NUTRITION

- Calories 320 cal
- Fat 12.4g
- Carbohydrates 18.5g
- Fiber 0.6g
- Protein 33.4g

PREPARATION: 15 MIN　　　**COOKING TIME: 16 MIN**　　　**SERVES: 2**

51. CHICKEN NUGGETS

INGREDIENTS

- 4-ounce boneless skinless chicken breast (cut into bite sizes)
- ½ teaspoon salt or to taste
- ½ cup bread crumbs
- ¼ teaspoon sugar
- 2 tablespoon buttermilk
- ½ lemon (squeezed)
- ½ teaspoon garlic powder
- ¼ ground black pepper
- ¼ teaspoon nutmeg
- A pinch of Italian seasoning

DIRECTIONS

1. Combine the chicken, sugar buttermilk and lemon in a bowl. Toss until well combined. Place the bowl in a refrigerator and marinate for about 2 hours.
2. Start your grill on smoke mode, leaving the lid opened for 5 minutes or until fire starts.
3. Close the lid and preheat the grill to 400°F for 5 minutes, using hickory hardwood pellet.
4. Grease a baking pan with non-stick spray.
5. Put the breadcrumbs in a bowl. Set aside.
6. Mix the pepper, salt, Italian seasoning and nutmeg in another bowl. Set aside.
7. Remove the chicken slices from the marinade and season with the seasoning mixture.
8. Dip each chicken piece into the breadcrumbs. Make sure all sides of each chicken piece are coated with breadcrumbs.
9. Arrange the coated chicken into the baking pan and press the chicken pieces to flatten them.
10. Place the baking pan directly on the grill and bake for 16 minutes or until chicken pieces turn golden brown.
11. Remove the chicken from the grill and let them cool for a few minutes.
12. Serve

NUTRITION

- Calories 231 cal
- Fat 6g
- Carbohydrates 22.7g

- Fiber 1.8g
- Protein 20.8g

52. HULI HULI CHICKEN

INGREDIENTS

- 4 pounds boneless skinless chicken thighs
- 1/3 cup ketchup
- 1 cup pineapple juice
- ½ cup soy sauce
- ½ cup brown sugar
- 2 tablespoon minced ginger
- 2 tablespoon Worcestershire sauce
- 2 garlic cloves (minced)
- Garnish:
- 4 tablespoon chopped green onions

DIRECTIONS

1. In a mixing bowl, combine the soy sauce, brown sugar, ketchup, soy sauce, ginger, ketchup, Worcestershire sauce, pineapple juice and garlic.
2. Pour 1 cup of the mixture into a gallon size zip-lock bag. Add the chicken thighs and massage the marinade into the thighs. Seal the bag and refrigerate for 1 hour.
3. Meanwhile, pour the remaining marinade mixture into a saucepan over medium to high heat. Bring to a boil, reduce the heat and simmer until the sauce thickens.
4. Remove the saucepan from heat.
5. Remove the thighs from the marinade and let them rest for about an hour or until they are at room temperature.
6. Preheat your grill to 250°F with lid closed for 10-15 minutes. Use apple hardwood pellets.
7. Arrange thighs on the grill grate and cook for 2 hours. Flip half way through.
8. Brush reserved sauce over chicken thighs generously. Cook for 30 minutes more or until the internal temperature of the thighs reaches 165°F.
9. Remove the wings from the heat and let them rest for a few minutes.
10. Serve and garnish with chopped green onions.

NUTRITION

- Calories 408 cal
- Fat 13.6g
- Carbohydrate 14.9g
- Fiber 0.3g
- Protein 53.7g

PREPARATION: 10 MIN	COOKING TIME: 16 MIN	SERVES: 6

53. HERB SMOKED CHICKEN

INGREDIENTS

- 3 tablespoon olive oil
- 1 teaspoon thyme
- 1 teaspoon ground black pepper or to taste
- 4 tablespoon freshly squeezed lemon juice
- 1 tablespoon lemon zest
- 1 tablespoon freshly chopped parsley
- 1 teaspoon salt or taste
- 1 tablespoon chopped rosemary
- 2 tablespoon freshly chopped cilantro
- 6 boneless chicken breasts

DIRECTIONS

1. In a large mixing bowl, combine the thyme, oil, pepper, juice, lemon zest, parsley, rosemary, cilantro and salt. Add the chicken breast and toss to combine. Cover the mixing bowl and refrigerate for 1 hour.
2. Remove the chicken breast from the marinade and let it rest for a few minutes, until it is at room temperature.
3. Start your grill on smoke, leaving the lid opened for 5 minutes or until fire starts.
4. Close the lid and preheat grill to 450°F with lid closed for 10-15 minutes, using mesquite wood pellets.
5. Arrange the chicken breasts onto the grill grate and smoke for 16 minutes, 8 minutes per side, or until the internal temperature of the chicken reaches 165°F.
6. Remove the chicken breasts from the grill and let them rest for a few minutes.
7. Serve and top with your favorite sauce.

NUTRITION

- Calories 207 cal
- Fat 11.2g
- Carbohydrate 1.2g
- Fiber 0.5g
- Protein 25.2g

CHAPTER 9
Seafood Recipes

PREPARATION: 10 MIN

COOKING TIME: 30 MIN

SERVES: 4

54. Roasted Yellowtail

INGREDIENTS

- 4 Yellowtail Filets (6 oz.)
- 1 lb. new Potatoes
- 2 tablespoon Olive oil
- 1 lb. Mushrooms, oyster
- 1 teaspoon ground Black pepper
- 4 tablespoon of olive oil

Salsa Verde:

- 1 tablespoon Cilantro, chopped
- 2 tablespoon Mint, chopped
- ½ cup Parsley, chopped
- 2 cloves of garlic, minced
- 1 tablespoon Oregano, chopped
- 1 Lemon, the juice
- 1 cup of Olive oil
- 1/8 teaspoon Pepper Flake
- Salt

- Calories: 398 cal
- Protein: 52g

DIRECTIONS

1. Preheat the grill to high with closed lid.
2. Place an iron pan directly on the grill. Heat it for 10 minutes.
3. Rub the fish with oil. Season with black pepper and salt.
4. In 2 different bowls place the mushrooms and potatoes, drizzle with oil and season with black pepper and salt. Toss.
5. Place the potatoes in the pan. Cook 10 minutes. Add the mushrooms.
6. Place the fillets on the grate with the skin down. Cook for 6 minutes and flip. Cook for 4 minutes more.
7. While the potatoes, mushrooms, and fish are cooking make the Salsa Verde. In a bowl combine all the ingredients and stir to combine.
8. Place the mushrooms and potatoes on a plate, top with a fillet and drizzle with the Salsa Verde.

NUTRITION

- Carbohydrates: 20g
- Fat: 18g

- Fiber 0g

PREPARATION: 15 MIN

COOKING TIME: 20 MIN

SERVES: 4-6

55. Baked Steelhead

INGREDIENTS

- 1 Lemon
- 2 Garlic cloves, minced
- ½ Shallot, minced
- 3 tablespoon Butter, unsalted
- Saskatchewan seasoning, blackened
- Italian Dressing
- 1 Steelhead, (a fillet)

DIRECTIONS

1. Preheat the grill to 350F with closed lid.
2. In an iron pan place the butter. Place the pan in the grill while preheating so that the butter melts. Coat the fillet with Italian dressing. Rub with Saskatchewan rub. Make sure the layer is thin.
3. Mince the garlic and shallot. Remove the pan from the grill and add the garlic and shallots.
4. Spread the mixture on the fillet. Slice the lemon into slices. Place the slice on the butter mix.
5. Place the fish on the grate. Cook 20 - 30 minutes.

NUTRITION

- Calories: 230
- Protein: 28g
- Fiber: 0g

- Carbohydrates 2g
- Fat: 14g

PREPARATION: 20 MIN

COOKING TIME: 25 MIN

SERVES: 8

56. FISH STEW

INGREDIENTS

- 1 jar (28oz.) Crushed Tomatoes
- 2 oz. of Tomato paste
- ¼ cup of White wine
- ¼ cup of Chicken Stock
- 2 tablespoon Butter
- 2 Garlic cloves, minced
- ¼ Onion, diced
- ½ lb. Shrimp divined and cleaned
- ½ lb. of Clams
- ½ lb. of Halibut
- Parsley
- Bread

DIRECTIONS

1. Preheat the grill to 300F with closed lid.
2. Place a Dutch oven over medium heat and melt the butter.
3. Sauté the onion for 4 - 7 minutes. Add the garlic. Cook 1 more minute.
4. Add the tomato paste. Cook until the color becomes rust red. Pour the stock and wine. Cook 10 minutes. Add the tomatoes, simmer.
5. Chop the halibut and together with the other seafood add in the Dutch oven. Place it on the grill and cover with a lid.
6. Let it cook for 20 minutes.
7. Season with black pepper and salt and set aside.
8. Top with chopped parsley and serve with bread.

NUTRITION

- Calories: 188
- Protein: 25g
- Carbohydrates: 7g
- Fiber: 2.9g
- Fat: 12g

PREPARATION: 15 MIN

COOKING TIME: 25 MIN

SERVES: 6

57. WHOLE VERMILLION SNAPPER

INGREDIENTS

- 2 Rosemary springs
- 4 Garlic cloves, chopped (peeled)
- 1 Lemon, thinly sliced
- Black pepper
- Sea Salt
- 1 Vermillion Snapper, gutted and scaled

DIRECTIONS

1. Preheat the grill to high with closed lid.
2. Stuff the fish with garlic. Sprinkle with rosemary, black pepper, sea salt and stuff with lemon slices.
3. Grill for 25 minutes.

NUTRITION

- Calories: 240
- Protein: 43g
- Carbohydrates: 0g
- Fat: 3g
- Fiber: 0g

PREPARATION: 10 MIN	COOKING TIME: 40 MIN	SERVES: 4

58. Smoked Sea Bass

INGREDIENTS

Marinade
- 1 teaspoon Blackened Saskatchewan
- 1 tablespoon Thyme, fresh
- 1 tablespoon Oregano, fresh
- 8 cloves of Garlic, crushed
- 1 lemon, the juice
- ¼ cup oil
- Sea Bass

- 4 Sea bass fillets, skin off

Chicken Rub Seasoning
- Seafood seasoning (like Old Bay)
- 8 tablespoon Gold Butter
- For garnish
- Thyme
- Lemon

DIRECTIONS

1. Make the marinade: In a Ziploc bag combine the ingredients and mix. Add the fillets and marinate for 30 min in the fridge. Turn once.
2. Preheat the grill to 325F with closed lid.
3. In a dish for baking add the butter. Remove the fish from marinade and pour it in the baking dish. Season the fish with chicken and seafood rub. Place it in the baking dish and on the grill. Cook 30 minutes. Baste 1 - 2 times.
4. Remove from the grill when the internal temperature is 160F.
5. Garnish with lemon slices and thyme.

NUTRITION

- Calories: 220
- Protein: 32g
- Carbohydrates: 1g
- Fiber: 0g
- Fat: 8g

PREPARATION: 10 MIN	COOKING TIME: 15 MIN	SERVES: 4-6

59. Tuna Burgers

INGREDIENTS

- 2 lbs. Tuna steak, ground
- 2 Eggs
- 1 Bell pepper, diced
- 1 teaspoon Worcestershire or soy sauce
- 1 Onion, Diced
- 1 tablespoon Salmon rub seasoning
- 1 tablespoon Saskatchewan Seasoning

DIRECTIONS

1. In a large bowl combine the salmon seasoning, Saskatchewan seasoning, bell pepper, onion, soy/Worcestershire sauce, eggs, and tuna. Mix well. Oil the hands, make patties.
2. Preheat the grill to high.
3. Grill the tuna patties for 10 - 15 min. Flip after 7 minutes.

NUTRITION

- Calories: 236
- Protein: 18g
- Carbohydrates: 1g
- Fat: 5g
- Fiber: 0.7g

PREPARATION: 10 MIN

COOKING TIME: 8 MIN

SERVES: 6-8

60. GRILLED CLAMS WITH GARLIC BUTTER

INGREDIENTS

- 1 Lemon, cut wedges
- 1 - 2 teaspoon Anise - flavored Liqueur
- 2 tablespoon Parsley, minced
- 2 - 3 Garlic cloves, minced
- 8 tablespoon butter, chunks
- 24 of Littleneck Clams

DIRECTIONS

1. Clean the clams with cold water. Discard those who are with broken shells or don't close.
2. Preheat the grill to 450F with closed lid.
3. In a casserole dish squeeze juice from 2 wedges, and add parsley, garlic, butter, and liqueur. Arrange the littleneck clams on the grate. Grill 8 minutes, until open. Discard those that won't open.
4. Transfer the clams in the baking dish.
5. Serve in a shallow dish with lemon wedges. Enjoy!

NUTRITION

- Calories: 273
- Protein: 4g
- Carbohydrates: 0.5g

- Fiber: 0g

PREPARATION: 45 MIN

COOKING TIME: 10 MIN

SERVES: 4-6

61. SIMPLE BUT DELICIOUS FISH RECIPE

INGREDIENTS

- 4 lbs. fish cut it into pieces (portion size)
- 1 tablespoon minced Garlic
- 1/3 cup of Olive oil
- 1 cup of Soy Sauce
- Basil, chopped
- 2 Lemons, the juice

DIRECTIONS

1. Preheat the grill to 350F with closed lid.
2. Combine the ingredients in a bowl. Stir to combine. Marinade the fish for 45 min.
3. Grill the fish until it reaches 145F internal temperature.
4. Serve with your favorite side dish and enjoy!

NUTRITION

- Calories: 153
- Protein: 25g
- Carbohydrates: 1g

- Fiber: 0.3g
- Fat: 4g

PREPARATION: 15 MIN

COOKING TIME: 30 MIN

SERVES: 4-6

62. Crab Legs On The Grill

INGREDIENTS

- 1 cup melted Butter
- 3 lb. Halved Crab Legs
- 2 tablespoon Lemon juice, fresh
- 1 tablespoon Old Bay
- 2 Garlic cloves, minced
- For garnish, chopped parsley
- For serving: Lemon wedges

DIRECTIONS

1. Place the crab legs in a roasting pan.
2. In a bowl combine the lemon juice, butter, and garlic. Mix. Pour over the legs. Coat well. Sprinkle with old bay.
3. Preheat the grill to 350F with closed lid.
4. Place the roasting pan on the grill and cook 20 - 30 minutes busting two times with the sauce in the pan.
5. Place the legs on a plate. Divide the crab sauce among 4 bowls for dipping.

NUTRITION

- Calories: 170
- Proteins: 20g
- Carbohydrates: 0
- Fiber: 0g
- Fat: 8g

PREPARATION: 10 MIN

COOKING TIME: 16 MIN

SERVES: 6-8

63. Garlic Salmon

INGREDIENTS

- 1 skin - on Salmon Filet
- 2 tablespoon Garlic, minced
- 1 bottle BBQ Sauce
- 4 Green onions sprigs, chopped
- Salmon Seasoning

DIRECTIONS

1. Season the fish with Salmon seasoning.
2. In a bowl add the BBQ sauce, 2 springs green onion (chopped), and garlic.
3. Stir well to combine and set aside.
4. Preheat the grill to 450F with closed lid.
5. Brush the fish with the sauce mixture. Grill with the skin down for 8 min per side.
6. Serve sprinkled with green onion. Enjoy!

NUTRITION

- Calories: 240
- Proteins: 23g
- Carbohydrates: 3g
- Fat: 16g
- Fiber: 0g

PREPARATION: 5 MIN

COOKING TIME: 5 MIN

SERVES: 2-4

64. SEARED TUNA STEAKS

INGREDIENTS

- 3 -inch Tuna
- Black pepper
- Sea Salt
- Olive oil
- Sriracha
- Soy Sauce

DIRECTIONS

1. Baste the tuna steaks with oil and sprinkle with black pepper and salt.
2. Preheat the grill to high with closed lid.
3. Grill the tuna for 2 ½ minutes per side.
4. Remove from the grill. Let it rest for 5 minutes.
5. Cut into thin pieces and serve with Sriracha and Soy Sauce. Enjoy.

NUTRITION

- Calories: 120
- Proteins: 34g
- Carbohydrates: 0g
- Fiber: 0g
- Fat: 1.5g

PREPARATION: 30 MIN

COOKING TIME: 1 H 30 MIN

SERVES: 8-12

65. ROASTED SHRIMP MIX

INGREDIENTS

- 3 lb. Shrimp (large), with tails, divided
- 2 lb. Kielbasa Smoked Sausage
- 6 corns cut into 3 pieces
- 2 lb. Potatoes, red
- Old Bay

DIRECTIONS

1. Preheat the grill to 275F with closed lid.
2. First, cook the sausage on the grill. Cook for 1 hour.
3. Increase the temperature to high. Season the corn and potatoes with Old Bay. Now roast until they become tender.
4. Season the shrimp with the Old Bay and cook on the grill for 20 minutes.
5. In a bowl combine the cooked ingredients. Toss.
6. Adjust seasoning with Old Bay and serve. Enjoy!

NUTRITION

- Calories: 530
- Proteins: 20g
- Carbohydrates: 32g
- Fat: 35g
- Fiber: 1g

PREPARATION: 10 MIN

COOKING TIME: 35 MIN

SERVES: 4

66. SEASONED SHRIMP SKEWERS

INGREDIENTS

- 1 ½ pound fresh large shrimp, peeled, deveined and rinsed
- 2 tablespoons minced basil
- 2 teaspoons minced garlic
- 1/2 teaspoon sea salt
- 1/2 teaspoon ground black pepper
- 1/3 cup olive oil
- 2 tablespoons lemon juice

DIRECTIONS

1. Place basil, garlic, salt, black pepper and oil in a large bowl, whisk until well combined, then add shrimps and toss until well coated.
2. Then plug in the smoker, fill its tray with hickory woodchips and water pan with water and white wine halfway through, and place dripping pan above the water pan.
3. Then open the top vent, shut with lid and use temperature settings to preheat smoker at 225 degrees F.
4. In the meantime, thread shrimps on wooden skewers, six shrimps on each skewer.
5. Place shrimp skewers on smoker rack, then shut with lid and set the timer to smoke for 35 minutes or shrimps are opaque.
6. When done, drizzle lemon juice over shrimps and serve.

NUTRITION

- Calories: 168 Cal
- Carbohydrates: 2 g
- Fat: 11 g
- Protein: 14 g
- Fiber: 0 g

PREPARATION: 7 HOURS

COOKING TIME: 3 HOURS

SERVES: 8

67. MARINATED TROUT

INGREDIENTS

- 4 pounds trout fillets
- 1/2 cup salt
- 1/2 cup brown sugar
- 2 quarts water

DIRECTIONS

1. Pour water in a large container with lid, add salt and sugar and stir until salt and sugar are dissolved completely.
2. Add trout, pour in more water to submerge trout in brine and refrigerate for 4 to 8 hours, covering the container.
3. Then remove trout from brine, rinse well and pat dry with paper towels.
4. Place trout on a cooling rack, skin side down, and cool in the refrigerator for 2 hours or until dried.
5. Then remove trout from the refrigerator and bring to room temperature.
6. In the meantime, plug in the smoker, fill its tray with maple woodchips and water pan halfway through, and place dripping pan above the water pan.
7. Then open the top vent, shut with lid and use temperature settings to preheat smoker at 160 degrees F.
8. In the meantime,
9. Place trout on smoker rack, insert a meat thermometer, then shut with lid and set the timer to smoke for 2 ½ to 3 hours or more until meat thermometer registers an internal temperature of 145 degrees F.
10. Check vent of smoker every hour and add more woodchips and water to maintain temperature and smoke.
11. Serve straightaway.

NUTRITION

- Calories: 49 Cal
- Carbohydrates: 0 g
- Fat: 1.2 g
- Protein: 8.8 g
- Fiber: 0 g.

CHAPTER 10
Vegetable Recipes

PREPARATION: 20 MIN

COOKING TIME: 2 H 10 MIN

SERVES: 6

68. PERFECTLY SMOKED ARTICHOKE HEARTS

INGREDIENTS

- 12 canned whole artichoke hearts
- 1/4 cup of extra virgin olive oil
- 4 cloves of garlic minced
- 2 Tablespoon of fresh parsley finely chopped (leaves)
- 1 Tablespoon of fresh lemon juice freshly squeezed
- Salt to taste
- Lemon for garnish

DIRECTIONS

1. Start the pellet grill on SMOKE with the lid open until the fire is established. Set the temperature to 350 ⊠ and preheat, lid closed, for 10 to 15 minutes.
2. In a bowl, combine all remaining ingredients and pour over artichokes.
3. Place artichokes on a grill rack and smoke for 2 hours or so.
4. Serve hot with extra olive oil, and lemon halves.

NUTRITION

- Calories: 105.5
- Carbohydrates: 19g
- Fat: 0.5g

- Fiber: 11g
- Protein: 7.7g

PREPARATION: 15 MIN

COOKING TIME: 2 HOURS

SERVES: 6

69. FINELY SMOKED RUSSET POTATOES

INGREDIENTS

- 8 large Russet potatoes
- 1/2 cup of garlic-infused olive oil
- Kosher salt and black pepper to taste

DIRECTIONS

1. Start the pellet grill on SMOKE with the lid open until the fire is established. Set the temperature to 225 ⊠ and preheat, lid closed, for 10 to 15 minutes.
2. Rinse and dry your potatoes; pierce with a fork on all sides.
3. Drizzle with garlic-infused olive oil and rub generously all your potatoes with the salt and pepper.
4. Place the potatoes on the pellet smoker and close the lid.
5. Smoke potatoes for about 2 hours.
6. Serve hot with your favorite dressing.

NUTRITION

- Calories: 384
- Carbohydrates: 48g
- Fat: 18.2g

- Fiber: 3.7g
- Protein: 6g

PREPARATION: 15 MIN

COOKING TIME: 55 MIN

SERVES: 4

70. SIMPLE SMOKED GREEN CABBAGE (PELLET)

INGREDIENTS

- 1 medium head of green cabbage
- 1/2 cup of olive oil
- Salt and ground white pepper to taste

DIRECTIONS

1. Start the pellet grill on SMOKE with the lid open until the fire is established. Set the temperature to 250 ⊠ and preheat, lid closed, for 10 to 15 minutes.
2. Clean and rinse cabbage under running water.
3. Cut the stem and then cut it in half, then each half in 2 to 3 pieces.
4. Season generously cabbage with the salt and white ground pepper; drizzle with olive oil.
5. Arrange the cabbage peace on their side on a smoker tray and cover.
6. Smoke the cabbage for 20 minutes per side.
7. Remove cabbage and let rest for 5 minutes.
8. Serve immediately.

NUTRITION

- Calories: 57
- Carbohydrates: 13g
- Fat: 0.2g

- Fiber: 6g
- Protein: 3g

PREPARATION: 10 MIN

COOKING TIME: 1 HOUR

SERVES: 3

71. SMOKED ASPARAGUS WITH PARSLEY AND GARLIC

INGREDIENTS

- 1 bunch of fresh asparagus, cleaned
- 1 Tablespoon of finely chopped parsley
- 1 Tablespoon of minced garlic
- 1/2 cup of olive oil
- Salt and ground black pepper to taste

DIRECTIONS

1. Start the pellet grill on SMOKE with the lid open until the fire is established. Set the temperature to 225 ⊠ and preheat, lid closed, for 10 to 15 minutes.
2. Rinse and cut the ends off of the asparagus.
3. In a bowl, combine olive oil, chopped parsley, minced garlic, and the salt and pepper.
4. Season your asparagus with olive oil mixture.
5. Place the asparagus on a heavy-duty foil and fold the sides.
6. Smoke for 55 to 60 minutes or until soft (turn every 15 minutes).
7. Serve hot.

NUTRITION

- Calories: 352
- Carbohydrates: 6.7g
- Fat: 36.2g

- Fiber: 3.1g
- Protein: 3.4g

PREPARATION: 15 MIN	COOKING TIME: 1 H 40 MIN	SERVES: 4

72. SMOKED CORN COB WITH SPICY RUB

INGREDIENTS

- 10 ears of fresh sweet corn on the cob
- 1/2 cup of macadamia nut oil
- Kosher salt and fresh ground black pepper to taste
- 1/2 teaspoon of garlic powder
- 1/2 teaspoon of hot paprika flakes
- 1/2 teaspoon of dried parsley
- 1/4 teaspoon of ground mustard

DIRECTIONS

1. Start the pellet grill on SMOKE with the lid open until the fire is established. Set the temperature to 350 ⊠ and preheat, lid closed, for 10 to 15 minutes.
2. Combine macadamia nut oil with garlic powder, hot paprika flakes, dried parsley, and ground mustard.
3. Rub your corn with macadamia nut oil mixture and place on a grill rack.
4. Smoke corn for 80 to 90 minutes.
5. Serve hot.

NUTRITION

- Calories: 248
- Carbohydrates: 25g
- Fat: 15g

- Fiber: 3.2g
- Protein: 4.4g

PREPARATION: 15 MIN	COOKING TIME: 2 H	SERVES: 6

73. SMOKED SWEET PIE PUMPKINS

INGREDIENTS

- 4 small pie pumpkins
- Avocado oil to taste

DIRECTIONS

1. Start the pellet grill on SMOKE with the lid open until the fire is established. Set the temperature to 250 ⊠ and preheat, lid closed, for 10 to 15 minutes.
2. Cut pumpkins in half, top to bottom, and drizzle with avocado oil.
3. Place pumpkin halves on the smoker away from the fire.
4. Smoke pumpkins from 1 1/2 to 2 hours.
5. Remove pumpkins from smoked and allow to cool.
6. Serve to taste.

NUTRITION

- Calories: 167.1
- Carbohydrates: 10g
- Fat: 14.2g

- Fiber: 1g
- Protein: 1.7g

PREPARATION: 15 MIN

COOKING TIME: 1 H

SERVES: 6

74. SMOKED VEGETABLE "POTPOURRI" (PELLET)

INGREDIENTS

- 2 large zucchini sliced
- 2 red bell peppers sliced
- 2 Russet potatoes sliced
- 1 red onion sliced
- 1/2 cup of olive oil
- Salt and ground black pepper to taste

DIRECTIONS

1. Start the pellet grill on SMOKE with the lid open until the fire is established. Set the temperature to 350 ▨ and preheat, lid closed, for 10 to 15 minutes.
2. In the meantime, rinse and slice all vegetables; pat dry on a kitchen paper.
3. Generously season with the salt and pepper, and drizzle with olive oil.
4. Place your sliced vegetables into grill basket or onto grill rack and smoke for 40 to 45 minutes.
5. Serve hot.

NUTRITION

- Calories: 330.1
- Carbohydrates: 29g
- Fat: 21.6g

- Fiber: 4g
- Protein: 4.6g

PREPARATION: 10 MIN

COOKING TIME: 120 MIN

SERVES: 5

75. SMOKED HEALTHY CABBAGE

INGREDIENTS

- 1 head cabbage, cored
- 4 tablespoons butter
- 2 tablespoons rendered bacon fat
- 1 chicken bouillon cube
- 1 teaspoon fresh ground black pepper
- 1 garlic clove, minced

DIRECTIONS

1. Pre-heat your smoker to 240 degrees Fahrenheit using your preferred wood
2. Fill the hole of your cored cabbage with butter, bouillon cube, bacon fat, pepper and garlic
3. Wrap the cabbage in foil about two-thirds of the way up
4. Make sure to leave the top open
5. Transfer to your smoker rack and smoke for 2 hours
6. Unwrap and enjoy!

NUTRITION

- Calories: 231 cal
- Fats: 10g
- Carbohydrates: 26g

- Fiber: 1g
- Protein: 0g

PREPARATION: 15 MIN

COOKING TIME: 90 MIN

SERVES: 4

76. GARLIC AND ROSEMARY POTATO WEDGES

INGREDIENTS

- 4-6 large russet potatoes, cut into wedges
- ¼ cup olive oil
- 2 garlic cloves, minced
- 2 tablespoons rosemary leaves, chopped
- 2 teaspoon salt
- 1 teaspoon fresh ground black pepper
- 1 teaspoon sugar
- 1 teaspoon onion powder

- Calories: 291 cal
- Fats: 10g

DIRECTIONS

1. Pre-heat your smoker to 250 degrees Fahrenheit using maple wood
2. Take a large bowl and add potatoes and olive oil
3. Toss well
4. Take another small bowl and stir garlic, salt, rosemary, pepper, sugar, onion powder
5. Sprinkle the mix on all sides of the potato wedge
6. Transfer the seasoned wedge to your smoker rack and smoke for 1 and ½ hours
7. Serve and enjoy!

NUTRITION

- Carbohydrates: 46g
- Fiber: 2g

- Protein: 0g

PREPARATION: 5 MIN

COOKING TIME: 60 MIN

SERVES: 4

77. SMOKED TOMATO AND MOZZARELLA DIP

INGREDIENTS

- 8 ounces smoked mozzarella cheese, shredded
- 8 ounces Colby cheese, shredded
- ½ cup parmesan cheese, grated
- 1 cup sour cream
- 1 cup sun-dried tomatoes
- 1 and ½ teaspoon salt
- 1 teaspoon fresh ground pepper
- 1 teaspoon dried basil
- 1 teaspoon dried oregano
- 1 teaspoon red pepper flakes
- 1 garlic clove, minced
- ½ teaspoon onion powder
- French toast, serving

- Calories: 174 cal
- Fats: 11g
- Carbohydrates: 15g

DIRECTIONS

1. Pre-heat your smoker to 275 degrees Fahrenheit using your preferred wood
2. Take a large bowl and stir in the cheeses, tomatoes, pepper, salt, basil, oregano, red pepper flakes, garlic, onion powder and mix well
3. Transfer the mix to a small metal pan and transfer to a smoker
4. Smoke for 1 hour
5. Serve with toasted French bread

NUTRITION

- Fiber: 2g
- Protein: 0g

PREPARATION: 15 MIN

 COOKING TIME: 10 MIN

 SERVES: 4

78. Feisty Roasted Cauliflower

INGREDIENTS

- 1 cauliflower head, cut into florets
- 1 tablespoon oil
- 1 cup parmesan, grated
- 2 garlic cloves, crushed
- ½ teaspoon pepper
- ½ teaspoon salt
- ¼ teaspoon paprika

DIRECTIONS

1. Pre-heat your Smoker to 180 degrees F
2. Transfer florets to smoker and smoke for 1 hour
3. Take a bowl and add all ingredients except cheese
4. Once smoking is done, remove florets
5. Increase temperature to 450 degrees F, brush florets with the brush and transfer to grill
6. Smoke for 10 minutes more
7. Sprinkle cheese on top and let them sit (Lid closed) until cheese melts
8. Serve and enjoy!

NUTRITION

- Calories: 45 cal
- Fats: 2g
- Carbohydrates: 7g

- Protein: 0g
- Fiber: 1g

CHAPTER 11

Dessert Recipes

PREPARATION: 15 MIN

COOKING TIME: 10 MIN

SERVES: 4-6

79. GRILLED FRUIT WITH CREAM

INGREDIENTS

- 2 halved Apricot
- 1 halved Nectarine
- 2 halved peaches
- ¼ cup of Blueberries
- ½ cup of Raspberries
- 2 tablespoon of Honey
- 1 orange, the peel
- 2 cups of Cream
- ½ cup of Balsamic Vinegar

DIRECTIONS

1. Preheat the grill to 400F with closed lid.
2. Grill the peaches, nectarines and apricots for 4 minutes on each side.
3. Place a pan over the stove and turn on medium heat. Add 2 tablespoon of honey, vinegar, and orange peel. Simmer until medium thick.
4. Add honey and cream in a bowl. Whip until it reaches a soft form.
5. Place the fruits on a serving plate. Sprinkle with berries. Drizzle with balsamic reduction.
6. Serve with cream.

NUTRITION

- Calories: 230 cal
- Protein: 3g
- Fiber: 0g
- Carbohydrates: 35g
- Fat: 3g

PREPARATION: 20 MIN

COOKING TIME: 30 MIN

SERVES: 4-6

80. APPLE PIE ON THE GRILL

INGREDIENTS

- ¼ cup of Sugar
- 4 Apples, sliced
- 1 tablespoon of Cornstarch
- 1 teaspoon Cinnamon, ground
- 1 Pie Crust, refrigerated, soften in according to the directions on the box
- ½ cup of Peach preserves

DIRECTIONS

1. Preheat the grill to 375F with closed lid.
2. In a bowl combine the cinnamon, cornstarch, sugar, and apples. Set aside.
3. Place the piecrust in a pie pan. Spread the preserves and then place the apples. Fold the crust slightly.
4. Place a pan on the grill (upside - down) so that you don't brill/bake the pie directly on the heat.
5. Cook 30 - 40 minutes. Once done, set aside to rest.
6. Serve and enjoy!

NUTRITION

- Calories: 160 cal
- Protein: 0.5g
- Fiber: 0g
- Carbohydrates: 35g
- Fat: 1g

PREPARATION: 10 MIN

COOKING TIME: 14 MIN

SERVES: 6

81. GRILLED LAYERED CAKE

INGREDIENTS

- 2 x pound cake
- 3 cups of whipped cream
- ¼ cup melted butter
- 1 cup of blueberries
- 1 cup of raspberries
- 1 cup sliced strawberries

DIRECTIONS

1. Preheat the grill to high with closed lid.
2. Slice the cake loaf (3/4 inch), about 10 per loaf. Brush both sides with butter.
3. Grill for 7 minutes on each side. Set aside.
4. Once cooled completely start layering your cake. Place cake, berries then cream.
5. Sprinkle with berries and serve.

NUTRITION

- Calories: 160 cal
- Protein: 2.3g
- Carbohydrates: 22g

- Fiber: 0g
- Fat: 6g

PREPARATION: 30 MIN

COOKING TIME: 30 MIN

SERVES: 8-12

82. CINNAMON SUGAR PUMPKIN SEEDS

INGREDIENTS

- 2 tablespoon sugar
- Seeds from a pumpkin
- 1 teaspoon cinnamon
- 2 tablespoon melted butter

DIRECTIONS

1. Add wood pellets to your smoker and follow your cooker's startup procedure. Preheat your smoker, with your lid closed, until it reaches 350.
2. Clean the seeds and toss them in the melted butter. Add them to the sugar and cinnamon. Spread them out on a baking sheet, place on the grill, and smoke for 25 minutes.
3. Serve.

NUTRITION

- Calories: 127 cal
- Protein: 5mg
- Carbohydrates: 15g

- Fiber: 0g
- Fat: 21g

PREPARATION: 30 MIN	COOKING TIME: 40 MIN	SERVES: 8

83. BLACKBERRY PIE

INGREDIENTS

- Butter, for greasing
- ½ cup all-purpose flour
- ½ cup milk
- 2 pints blackberries
- 2 cups sugar, divided
- 1 box refrigerated piecrusts
- 1 stick melted butter
- 1 stick of butter
- Vanilla ice cream

DIRECTIONS

1. Add wood pellets to your smoker and follow your cooker's startup procedure. Preheat your smoker, with your lid closed, until it reaches 375.
2. Butter a cast iron skillet.
3. Unroll a piecrust and lay it in the bottom and up the sides of the skillet. Use a fork to poke holes in the crust.
4. Lay the skillet on the grill and smoke for five minutes, or until the crust is browned. Set off the grill.
5. Mix 1 ½ c. of sugar, the flour, and the melted butter together. Add in the blackberries and toss everything together.
6. The berry mixture should be added to the skillet. The milk should be added on the top afterward. Sprinkle on half of the diced butter.
7. Unroll the second pie crust and lay it over the skillet. You can also slice it into strips and weave it on top to make it look like a lattice. Place the rest of the diced butter over the top. Sprinkle the rest of the sugar over the crust and place it skillet back on the grill.
8. Lower the lid and smoke for 15 to 20 minutes or until it is browned and bubbly. You may want to cover with some foil to keep it from burning during the last few minutes of cooking. Serve the hot pie with some vanilla ice cream.

NUTRITION

- Calories: 393 cal
- Protein: 4.25g
- Fiber: 0g
- Carbohydrates: 53.67g
- Fat: 18.75g

PREPARATION: 30 MIN

COOKING TIME: 20 MIN

SERVES: 6-8

84. S'mores Dip

INGREDIENTS

- 12 ounces semisweet chocolate chips
- ¼ cup milk
- 2 tablespoon melted salted butter
- 16 ounces marshmallows
- Apple wedges
- Graham crackers

DIRECTIONS

1. Add wood pellets to your smoker and follow your cooker's startup procedure. Preheat your smoker, with your lid closed, until it reaches 450.
2. Put a cast iron skillet on your grill and add in the milk and melted butter. Stir together for a minute.
3. Once it has heated up, top with the chocolate chips, making sure it makes a single layer. Place the marshmallows on top, standing them on their end and covering the chocolate.
4. Cover, and let it smoke for five to seven minutes. The marshmallows should be toasted lightly.
5. Take the skillet off the heat and serve with apple wedges and graham crackers.

NUTRITION

- Calories: 216.7 cal
- Protein: 2.7g
- Fiber: 0g
- Carbohydrates: 41g
- Fat: 4.7g

PREPARATION: 30 MIN

COOKING TIME: 1 HOUR

SERVES: 12-16

85. Ice Cream Bread

INGREDIENTS

- 1 ½ quart full-fat butter pecan ice cream, softened
- One teaspoon salt
- Two cups semisweet chocolate chips
- One cup sugar
- One stick melted butter
- Butter, for greasing
- 4 cups self-rising flour

DIRECTIONS

1. Add wood pellets to your smoker and follow your cooker's startup procedure. Preheat your smoker, with your lid closed, until it reaches 350.
2. Mix the salt, sugar, flour, and ice cream with an electric mixer set to medium for two minutes.
3. As the mixer is still running, add in the chocolate chips, beating until everything is blended.
4. Spray a Bundt pan or tube pan with cooking spray. If you choose to use a pan that is solid, the center will take too long to cook. That's why a tube or Bundt pan works best.
5. Add the batter to your prepared pan.
6. Set the cake on the grill, cover, and smoke for 50 minutes to an hour. A toothpick should come out clean.
7. Take the pan off of the grill. For 10 minutes., cool the bread. Remove carefully the bread from the pan and then drizzle it with some melted butter.

NUTRITION

- Calories: 148.7 cal
- Protein: 3.5g
- Fiber: 0g
- Carbohydrates: 27g
- Fat: 3g

PREPARATION: 30 MIN

COOKING TIME: 30 MIN

SERVES: 12

86. BACON CHOCOLATE CHIP COOKIES

INGREDIENTS

- 8 slices cooked and crumbled bacon
- 2 ½ teaspoon apple cider vinegar
- One teaspoon vanilla
- Two cup semisweet chocolate chips
- Two room temp eggs
- 1 ½ teaspoon baking soda
- One cup granulated sugar
- ½ teaspoon salt
- 2 ¾ cup all-purpose flour
- One cup light brown sugar
- 1 ½ stick softened butter

- Calories: 133 cal
- Protein: 2.6g
- Fiber: 0g

DIRECTIONS

1. Mix together salt, baking soda and flour.
2. Cream the sugar and the butter together. Lower the speed. Add in the eggs, vinegar, and vanilla.
3. Still on low, slowly add in the flour mixture, bacon pieces, and chocolate chips.
4. Add wood pellets to your smoker and follow your cooker's startup procedure. Preheat your smoker, with your lid closed, until it reaches 375.
5. Place some parchment on a baking sheet and drop a teaspoonful of cookie batter on the baking sheet. Let them cook on the grill, covered, for approximately 12 minutes or until they are browned. Enjoy.

NUTRITION

- Carbohydrates: 11.8g
- Fat: 9.2g

PREPARATION: 30 MIN

COOKING TIME: 30 MIN

SERVES: 12

87. CHOCOLATE CHIP COOKIES

INGREDIENTS

- 1 ½ cup chopped walnuts
- One teaspoon vanilla
- Two cup chocolate chips
- One teaspoon baking soda
- 2 ½ cups plain flour
- ½ teaspoon salt
- 1 ½ stick softened butter
- Two eggs
- One cup brown sugar
- ½ cup sugar

DIRECTIONS

1. Add wood pellets to your smoker and follow your cooker's startup procedure. Preheat your smoker, with your lid closed, until it reaches 350.
2. Mix together the baking soda, salt, and flour.
3. Cream the brown sugar, sugar, and butter. Mix in the vanilla and eggs until it comes together.
4. Slowly add in the flour while continuing to beat. Once all flour has been incorporated, add in the chocolate chips and walnuts. Using a spoon, fold into batter.
5. Place an aluminum foil onto grill. In an aluminum foil, drop spoonfuls of dough and bake for 17 minutes.

NUTRITION

- Calories: 66.5 cal
- Protein: 1.8g
- Fiber: 0g
- Carbohydrates: 5.9g
- Fat: 4.6g

PREPARATION: 30 MIN

COOKING TIME: 1 H 50 MIN

SERVES: 8

88. APPLE COBBLER

INGREDIENTS

- 8 Granny Smith apples
- One cup sugar
- One stick melted butter
- One teaspoon cinnamon
- Pinch salt
- ½ cup brown sugar
- Two eggs
- Two teaspoon baking powder
- Two c. plain flour
- 1 ½ cup sugar

DIRECTIONS

1. Peel and quarter apples, place into a bowl. Add in the cinnamon and one c. sugar. Stir well to coat and let it set for one hour.
2. Add wood pellets to your smoker and follow your cooker's startup procedure. Preheat your smoker, with your lid closed, until it reaches 350.
3. In a large bowl add the salt, baking powder, eggs, brown sugar, sugar, and flour. Mix until it forms crumbles.
4. Place apples into a Dutch oven. Add the crumble mixture on top and drizzle with melted butter.
5. Place on the grill and cook for 50 minutes.

NUTRITION

- Calories: 216.7 cal
- Protein: 2.7g
- Fiber: 0g
- Carbohydrates: 41g
- Fat: 4.7g

PREPARATION: 30 MIN

COOKING TIME: 1 H 20 MIN

SERVES: 8

89. PINEAPPLE CAKE

INGREDIENTS

- One cup sugar
- One tablespoon baking powder
- One cup buttermilk
- ½ teaspoon salt
- One jar maraschino cherries
- One stick butter, divided
- ¾ cup brown sugar
- One can pineapple slices
- 1 ½ cup flour

DIRECTIONS

1. Add wood pellets to your smoker and follow your cooker's startup procedure. Preheat your smoker, with your lid closed, until it reaches 350.
2. Take a medium-sized cast iron skillet, melt one half stick butter. Be sure to coat the entire skillet. Sprinkle brown sugar into a cast iron skillet.
3. Lay the sliced pineapple on top of the brown sugar. Put a cherry into each individual pineapple ring.
4. Mix together the salt, baking powder, flour, and sugar. Add in the eggs, one-half stick melted butter, and buttermilk. Whisk to combine.
5. Put the cake on the grill and cook for an hour.
6. Take off from the grill and let it set for ten minutes. Flip onto serving platter.

NUTRITION

- Calories: 120 cal
- Protein: 1g
- Fiber: 0g
- Carbohydrates: 18g
- Fat: 5g

PREPARATION: 15 MIN

COOKING TIME: 15 MIN

SERVES: 4

90. CARAMEL BANANAS

INGREDIENTS

- 1/3 cup chopped pecans
- ½ cup sweetened condensed milk
- 4 slightly green bananas
- ½ cup brown sugar
- 2 tablespoon corn syrup
- ½ cup butter

DIRECTIONS

1. Add wood pellet to your smoker and follow your cooker's startup procedure. Preheat your smoker, with the lid closed, until it reaches 350.
2. Place the milk, corn syrup, butter, and brown sugar into a heavy saucepan and bring to boil. For five minutes, simmer the mixture in low heat. Stir frequently.
3. Place the bananas with their peels on, on the grill and let them grill for five minutes. Flip and cook for five minutes more. Peels will be dark and might split.
4. Place on serving platter. Cut the ends off the bananas and split peel down the middle. Take the peel off the bananas and spoon caramel on top. Sprinkle with pecans.

NUTRITION

- Calories: 345 cal
- Protein: 11g
- Fiber: 3.1g
- Carbohydrates: 77g
- Fat: 1g

PREPARATION: 30 MIN

COOKING TIME: 50 MIN

SERVES: 8

91. APPLE PIE

INGREDIENTS

- One frozen pie crust, thawed
- ¼ cup sugar
- ¼ cup peach preserves
- 1 tablespoon cornstarch
- 5 apples, cored, sliced thin

DIRECTIONS

1. Add wood pellet to your smoker and follow your cooker's startup procedure. Preheat your smoker, with the lid closed, until it reaches 375.
2. Mix the cornstarch, sugar, and apples together. Set to the side.
3. Unroll the pie crust and put into a pie pan. Spread the peach preserves evenly on the crust. Lay the apples out onto the crust. Fold the crust over apples.
4. Place on baking sheet upside down on the grill. Place the pie pan on top and bake for 35 minutes. Cool for five minutes before slicing.

NUTRITION

- Calories: 320 cal
- Protein: 2g
- Carbohydrates: 47g
- Fiber: 5g
- Fat: 15g

CHAPTER 12
Sandwich and Burger Recipes

PREPARATION: 10 MIN

COOKING TIME: 55 MIN

SERVES: 4

922 GRILLED STEAK WITH AMERICAN CHEESE SANDWICH

INGREDIENTS

- 1 pound of beef steak.
- 1/2 teaspoon of salt to taste.
- 1/2 teaspoon of pepper to taste.
- 1 tablespoon of Worcestershire sauce.
- 2 tablespoons of butter.
- 1 chopped onion.
- 1/2 chopped green bell pepper.
- Salt and pepper to taste.
- 8 slices of American Cheese.
- 8 slices of white bread.
- 4 tablespoons of butter.

DIRECTIONS

1. Turn your Wood Pellet Smoker and Grill to smoke and fire up for about four to five minutes. Set the temperature of the grill to 450 degrees F and let it preheat for about ten to fifteen minutes with its lid closed.
2. Next, place a non-stick skillet on the griddle and preheat for about fifteen minutes until it becomes hot. Once hot, add in the butter and let melt. Once the butter melts, add in the onions and green bell pepper then cook for about five minutes until they become brown in color, set aside.
3. Next, still using the same pan on the griddle, add in the steak, Worcestershire sauce, salt, and pepper to taste then cook for about five to six minutes until it is cooked through. Add in the cooked bell pepper mixture; stir to combine then heat for another three minutes, set aside.
4. Use a sharp knife to slice the bread in half, butter each side then grill for about three to four minutes with its sides down. To assemble, add slices of cheese on each bread slice, top with the steak mixture then your favorite toppings, close the sandwich with another bread slice then serve.

NUTRITION

- Calories 589 cal
- Carbohydrates 28g
- Protein 24g
- Fat 41g
- Fiber 2g

PREPARATION: 15 MIN

COOKING TIME: 50 MIN

SERVES: 6

93. GROUND TURKEY BURGERS

INGREDIENTS

- 1 beaten egg
- 2/3 cup of bread crumbs.
- 1/2 cup of chopped celery
- 1/4 cup of chopped onion
- 1 tablespoon of minced parsley
- 1 teaspoon of Worcestershire sauce
- 1 teaspoon of dried oregano
- 1/2 teaspoon of salt to taste
- 1/4 teaspoon of pepper
- 1-1/4 pounds of lean ground turkey
- 6 hamburger buns
- Optional topping
- 1 sliced tomato
- 1 sliced onion
- Lettuce leaves

DIRECTIONS

1. Using a small mixing bowl, add in all the ingredients on the list aside from the turkey and buns then mix properly to combine. Add in the ground turkey then mix everything to combine. Feel free to use clean hands for this. Make about six patties of the mixture then set aside.
2. Preheat your Wood Pellet Smoker and Grill to 375 degrees F, place the turkey patties on the grill and grill for about forty-five minutes until its internal temperature reads 165 degrees F. to assemble, use a knife to split the bun into two, top with the prepared burger and your favorite topping then close with another half of the buns, serve.

NUTRITION

- Calories 293 cal
- Fat 11g
- Carbohydrate 27g
- Fiber 4g
- Protein 22g

PREPARATION: 10 MIN

COOKING TIME: 5 H 10 MIN

SERVES: 4

94. BBQ Shredded Beef Burger

INGREDIENTS

- 3 pounds of boneless chuck roast.
- Salt to taste
- Pepper to taste
- 2 tablespoons of minced garlic
- 1 cup of chopped onion
- 28 oz. of barbeque sauce
- 6 buns

DIRECTIONS

1. Set the temperature of the Wood Pellet Smoker and Grill to 250 degrees F then preheat for about fifteen minutes with its lid closed. Use a knife to trim off the excess fat present on the roast then place the meat on the preheated grill. Grill the roast for about three and a half hours until it attains an internal temperature of 160 degrees F.
2. Next, place the chuck roast in an aluminum foil, add in the garlic, onion, barbeque sauce, salt, and pepper then stir to coat. Place the roast bake on the grill and cook for another one and a half hour until an inserted thermometer reads 204 degrees F.
3. Once cooked, let the meat cool for a few minutes then shred with a fork. Fill the buns with the shredded beef then serve.

NUTRITION

- Calories 593 cal
- Fat 31g
- Carbohydrates 34g
- Fiber 1g
- Protein 44g

PREPARATION: 15 MIN

COOKING TIME: 1 H

SERVES: 4-6

95. Grilled Pork Burgers

INGREDIENTS

- 1 beaten egg
- 3/4 cup of soft breadcrumbs
- 3/4 cup of grated parmesan cheese
- 1 tablespoon of dried parsley
- 2 teaspoons of dried basil
- 1/2 teaspoon of salt to taste
- 1/2 teaspoon of garlic powder
- 1/4 teaspoon of pepper to taste
- 2 pounds of ground pork
- 6 hamburger buns
- Toppings
- Lettuce leaves
- Sliced tomato
- Sliced sweet onion

DIRECTIONS

1. Using a large mixing bowl, add in the egg, bread crumbs, cheese, parsley, basil, garlic powder, salt, and pepper to taste then mix properly to combine. Add in the ground pork then mix properly to combine using clean hands. Form about six patties out the mixture then set aside.
2. Next, set a Wood Pellet smoker and grill to smoke (250 degrees F) then let it fire up for about five minutes. Place the patties on the grill and smoke for about thirty minutes. Flip the patties over, increase the temperature of the grill to 300 degrees F then grill the patties for a few minutes until an inserted thermometer reads 160 degrees F.
3. Serve the pork burgers on the buns, lettuce, tomato, and onion.

NUTRITION

- Calories 522 cal
- Fat 28g
- Carbohydrate 28g
- Fiber 2g
- Protein 38g

| PREPARATION: 15 MIN | COOKING TIME: 35 MIN | SERVES: 4-6 |

96. Delicious BLT Sandwich

INGREDIENTS

- 8 slices of bacon
- 1/2 romaine heart
- 1 sliced tomato
- 4 slices of sandwich bread
- 3 tablespoons of mayonnaise
- Salted butter
- Sea salt to taste
- Pepper to taste

DIRECTIONS

1. Preheat a Wood Pellet Smoker and Grill to 350 degrees F for about fifteen minutes with its lid closed. Place the bacon slices on the preheated grill and cook for about fifteen to twenty minutes until they become crispy.
2. Next, butter both sides of the bread, place a grill pan on the griddle of the Pellet, and toast the bread for a few minutes until they become brown on both sides, set aside. Using a small mixing bowl, add in the sliced tomatoes, season with salt and pepper to taste then mix to coat.
3. Next, spread mayo on both sides of the toasted bread, top with the lettuce, tomato, and bacon then enjoy.

NUTRITION

- Calories 284 cal
- Protein 19g
- Fat 19g
- Carbohydrates 11g
- Fiber 2g

| PREPARATION: 15 MIN | COOKING TIME: 50 MIN | SERVES: 4 |

97. Delicious Grilled Chicken Sandwich

INGREDIENTS

- 1/4 cup of mayonnaise
- 1 tablespoon of Dijon mustard
- 1 tablespoon of honey
- 4 boneless and skinless chicken breasts
- 1/2 teaspoon of steak seasoning
- 4 slices of American Swiss cheese
- 4 hamburger buns
- 2 bacon strips
- Lettuce leaves and tomato slices

DIRECTIONS

1. Using a small mixing bowl, add in the mayonnaise, mustard, and honey then mix properly to combine. Use a meat mallet to pound the chicken into even thickness then slice into four parts. Season the chicken with the steak seasoning then set aside.
2. Preheat a Wood Pellet Smoker and Grill to 350 degrees F for about ten to fifteen minutes with its lid closed. Place the seasoned chicken on the grill and grill for about twenty-five to thirty minutes until it reads an internal temperature of 165 degrees F. Grill the bacon until crispy then crumble.
3. Add the cheese on the chicken and cook for about one minute until it melts completely. At the same time, grill the buns for about one to two minutes until it is toasted as desired. Place the chicken on the buns, top with the grilled bacon, mayonnaise mixture, lettuce, and tomato then serve.

NUTRITION

- Calories 410 cal
- Fat 17g
- Carbohydrate 29g
- Fiber 3g
- Protein 34g

PREPARATION: 15 MIN

COOKING TIME: 20 MIN

SERVES: 4

98. Bacon, Egg, And Cheese Sandwich

INGREDIENTS

- 2 large eggs
- 2 tablespoons of milk or water
- A pinch of salt to taste
- A pinch of pepper to taste
- 3 teaspoons of butter
- 4 slices of white bread
- 2 slices of Jack cheese
- 4 slices of bacon

DIRECTIONS

1. Using a small mixing bowl, add in the eggs, milk, salt, and pepper to taste then mix properly to combine. Preheat a Wood Pellet Smoker and Grill to 400 degrees F for about ten to fifteen minutes with its lid closed. Place the bacon slices on the preheated grill and grill for about eight to ten minutes, flipping once until it becomes crispy. Set the bacon aside on a paper-lined towel.
2. Decrease the temperature of the grill to 350 degrees F, place a grill pan on the grill, and let it heat for about ten minutes. Spread two tablespoons of butter on the cut side of the bread, place the bread on the skillet pan and toast for about two minutes until brown in color.
3. Place the cheese on the toasted bread, close the lid of the grill then cook for about one minute until the cheese melts completely, set aside. Still using the same grill pan, add in the rest of the butter then let melt. Pour in the egg mixture and cook for a few minutes until it is cooked as desired.
4. Assemble the sandwich as desired then serve.

NUTRITION

- Calories 401 cal
- Fat 23g
- Carbohydrates 26g
- Fiber 3g
- Protein 23g

PREPARATION: 15 MIN

COOKING TIME: 25 MIN

SERVES: 5

99. Grilled Lamb Burgers

INGREDIENTS

- 1 1/4 pounds of ground lamb.
- 1 egg
- 1 teaspoon of dried oregano
- 1 teaspoon of dry sherry
- 1 teaspoon of white wine vinegar
- 1/2 teaspoon of crushed red pepper flakes
- 4 minced cloves of garlic
- 1/2 cup of chopped green onions
- 1 tablespoon of chopped mint
- 2 tablespoons of chopped cilantro
- 2 tablespoons of dry bread crumbs
- 1/8 teaspoon of salt to taste
- 1/4 teaspoon of ground black pepper to taste
- 5 hamburger buns

DIRECTIONS

1. Preheat a Wood Pellet Smoker or Grill to 350-450 degrees F then grease it grates. Using a large mixing bowl, add in all the ingredients on the list aside from the buns then mix properly to combine with clean hands. Make about five patties out of the mixture then set aside.
2. Place the lamb patties on the preheated grill and cook for about seven to nine minutes turning only once until an inserted thermometer reads 160 degrees F. Serve the lamb burgers on the hamburger, add your favorite toppings and enjoy.

NUTRITION

- Calories: 376 cal
- Fat: 18.5g
- Fiber 1.6g
- Carbohydrates 25.4g
- Protein 25.5 g

PREPARATION: 15 MIN	COOKING TIME: 55 MIN	SERVES: 6

100. GRILLED LAMB SANDWICHES

INGREDIENTS

- 1 (4 pounds) boneless lamb
- 1 cup of raspberry vinegar
- 2 tablespoons of olive oil
- 1 tablespoon of chopped fresh thyme
- 2 pressed garlic cloves
- 1/4 teaspoon of salt to taste
- 1/4 teaspoon of ground pepper
- Sliced bread

DIRECTIONS

1. Using a large mixing bowl, add in the raspberry vinegar, oil, and thyme then mix properly to combine. Add in the lamb, toss to combine then let it sit in the refrigerator for about eight hours or overnight.
2. Next, discard the marinade the season the lamb with salt and pepper to taste. Preheat a Wood Pellet Smoker and grill t0 400-500 degrees F, add in the seasoned lamb and grill for about thirty to forty minutes until it attains a temperature of 150 degrees F.
3. Once cooked, let the lamb cool for a few minutes, slice as desired then serve on the bread with your favorite topping.

NUTRITION

- Calories 407 cal
- Fat 23g

- Carbohydrate 26g
- Fiber 2.3g

- Protein 72g

CHAPTER 13

Pizza Recipes

**PREPARATION: 15 MIN +
1½ TO 2 HOURS REST TIME)**

COOKING TIME: 15-20 MIN

SERVES: 4-6

101. PIZZA DOUGH ROLLS

INGREDIENTS

- 2½ cups bread flour or handy flour
- 1 teaspoon moment or fast ascent yeast
- 1 teaspoon fit salt
- 1 teaspoon sugar
- 1 cup warm water
- 1 tablespoon extra-virgin olive oil

DIRECTIONS

1. Preparing for the grill:
2. In a large bowl, join the flour, yeast, salt, and sugar.
3. Include the water and olive oil, and mix utilizing a wooden spoon until the mixture has a clingy, shaggy surface.
4. Manipulate the pizza batter gently for 3 to 4 minutes utilizing floured hands and spread with a flour-sack towel.
5. Let sit, secured, for 1 hour at room temperature. The mixture should double in size.
6. On a clean, dry, gently floured surface, partition the pizza batter into 8 equivalent segments. Structure each part into a move shape utilizing floured hands.
7. Spread a baking sheet or pizza dish with parchment paper, and place the moves on the paper. Spread the moves with a flour-sack towel.
8. Enable the moves to rise again for 30 to 60 minutes, until they double in size.
9. On the wood pellet smoker-grill:
10. Configure the wood pellet smoker-grill for a non-direct cooking and preheat to 400°F utilizing any pellets.
11. Utilize a couple of scissors to score a "X" on top of every pizza batter roll.
12. Place the parchment-secured sheet or skillet directly on the grill grates and bake for 15 to 20 minutes, until the moves are brilliant dark colored and the internal temperature estimated in the focal point of the moves arrives at 210°F.

NUTRITION

- Calories: 179.7 cal
- Fat: 4g

- Carbohydrate: 31.1g
- Fiber: 1.4g

- Protein: 4.4g

PREPARATION: 15 MIN

COOKING TIME: 30 MIN

SERVES: 4

102. BAKED GRILLED PIZZA

INGREDIENTS

- Pizza

DIRECTIONS

1. Pepping on the wood pellet smoker
2. Set the wood pellet smoker grill to indirect cooking and preheat to 400⊠F
3. Transfer the pizza to the fridge and refrigerate 2 hours
4. Remove and prepare the smoker
5. Place the pizza into the grill grates and allow baking for 15 minutes or until the pizza crust turns brown
6. Remove it from the grill and allow resting for 10 minutes
7. Slice, serve and enjoy

NUTRITION

- Calories: 282.4 cal
- Fat: 13g

- Carbohydrate: 23.8g
- Fiber: 1.8g

- Protein: 18.2g

CHAPTER 14

The real Pit Master meal plan

WEEK 1	
MONDAY	Smoked Avocado Pork Ribs
TUESDAY	Grilled Almond-Crusted Beef Fillet
WEDNESDAY	Roasted Leg Of Lamb
THURSDAY	Tempting Tarragon Turkey Breasts
FRIDAY - BURGER DAY!	BBQ Shredded Beef Burger
SATURDAY	Smoked Chicken Drumsticks
SUNDAY	Roasted Yellowtail
SUNDAY DESSERT	Grilled Fruit With Cream

WEEK 2	
MONDAY	Smoked Honey - Garlic Pork Chops
TUESDAY	Grilled Beef Eye Fillet With Herb Rubs
WEDNESDAY	Greek-Style Roast Leg Of Lamb
THURSDAY	Juicy Beer Can Turkey
FRIDAY - PIZZA DAY!	Baked Grilled Pizza
SATURDAY	Baked Steelhead
SUNDAY	Smoked Chicken Leg Quarters
SUNDAY DESSERT	Chocolate Chip Cookies

WEEK 3	
MONDAY	Smoked Pork Loin In Sweet-Beer Marinade
TUESDAY	Rosemary Lamb
WEDNESDAY	Jalapeno Injection Turkey
THURSDAY	Grilled Beef Steaks With Beer-Honey Sauce
FRIDAY - BURGER DAY!	Bacon, Egg, And Cheese Sandwich
SATURDAY	Grilled Chicken Kebabs
SUNDAY	Garlic Salmon
SUNDAY DESSERT	Caramel Bananas

WEEK 4	
MONDAY	Grilled Clams With Garlic Butter
TUESDAY	Smoked Pork Cutlets With Caraway And Dill
WEDNESDAY	Herb Smoked Chicken
THURSDAY	Buttered Thanksgiving Turkey
FRIDAY - PIZZA DAY!	Pizza Dough Rolls
SATURDAY	Chicken Nuggets
SUNDAY	Smoked Pork Chops Marinated With Tarragon
SUNDAY DESSERT	Ice Cream Bread

Now you can organize your meals, even during the holidays. Everything will be simpler. Also, here are a couple of tips to make the most of it:

1. If you want, for each meal shown, you can choose your favorite sauce from chapter three.

2. You can combine the different recipes of this meal plan for a total of 2000 days and more, without getting bored (I give you my word!).

3. Havefuneverytimeyouareinfrontofyourpitboss–It'ssuchasecretingredients!

CONCLUSION

Ultimately, the decision about the best barbecue books to buy as your guides to barbecuing will depend mainly on your own personal preferences. However, this cookbook serves as a guide that will be good for the majority of people to get into the more elaborate styles of barbecue. More importantly, this guide presents some of the more intricate details of smoking in an easy-to-understand way. This guide is one that you can grow with as you become more confident in barbecuing. You have obtained every secret to cooking with a Wood Pellet Smoker-Grill, and you have tons of great recipes to try again and again. Plus, with this smoker-grill, you can expect the same delicious flavors every single time. All you need to do is follow the ingredients and directions accurately. You have many different kinds of recipes, so you can try a new dish every day and test your cooking skills. Practicing will improve your ability to obtain great flavors.

To start cooking, go through the process of using your Wood Pellet Smoker-Grill and understanding the benefits, so you can leverage the equipment to its fullest ability when cooking. After that, you can pick your favorite recipes from the segments of lamb, beef, pork, and seafood. Start by trying the recipes from different categories. That way, you will be trying different directions of cooking, such as smoking, grilling, searing, and more. The presented instructions are simple, so you need to follow them.

I am very optimistic that you are well acquainted with some of the most excellent smoker grill recipes which will make you a pro at grilling, BBQ, and cooking in general. The recipes in this book are well-chosen and are surely the best. I invested a lot of passion, energy, and time in this cookbook to make sure that each recipe is as exquisite as I desired these to be. This cookbook greatly matches the outstanding culinary skills you acquire. If you put a smoker to the right use and use the best kind of pellets, the flavor is so delicious wherein everyone trying the food is filled with astonishment.

This book is categorized into different parts in which the recipes are similar to in order for you to view the recipes better. So, go through the book if and when you need it, make sure you follow the instructions in the recipe thoroughly. Stick to the specific details and follow the methods accurately in order to achieve the smoking best results. Despite so, you are free to modify and experiment the recipes written in this book in events that you do not have some of the ingredients.

Now, get the best out of this cookbook and explore the various recipes written in this book. Thank you for reading this book. I hope you'll enjoy every recipes and this meal plan. If you like to leave your review, i will be grateful and happy!

Made in United States
Troutdale, OR
04/21/2024